Rough edges

Christians living abroad

Rhena Taylor

© Rhena Taylor, 1978

First Printing, 1978
Second Printing, 1979

Reprinted 2004 with permission of author

ISBN 0 938978 209

Printed by Wycliffe Bible Translators
P.O. Box 628200
Orlando, FL
32862-8200

To order additional copies of
Rough Edges,
contact
Wycliffe's Media Resource Center
1-800-992-5433
media_resource_center@wycliffe.org

Contents

1	Requiem	1
2	The Yardstick	21
3	The Strike	39
4	The Love-Match	55
5	The Last Night	71
6	An Axe at the Roots	79
7	Between the Lines	97
8	The Triangle Again	119
9	Heartbreak	139
10	Death of a Cow	147
	For Further Thought	155

Thanks

We are most grateful to Rhena Taylor for granting permission to reprint *Rough Edges*. In many ways, the world has changed since this book was first published in 1978; yet the issues addressed are still very relevant and worthy of consideration by Christians working in a cross-cultural context.

Preface

Close interaction with other people, especially those of a different culture and race, almost inevitably causes stress, and often open conflict. These ten stories—fiction based on fact and loosely set "in Africa"—illustrate some of the situations in which this tension is apparent in today's missionary world. They are written in the belief that the answer is not to draw further away from each other and nurse our "rough edges," but to come closer together and so discover something new about the love of God.

RT.

Chapter 1
Requiem

Marcus Nkondi turned over again on the hard, narrow bed, burying his head despairingly in his bare arms. The lights always burned all night in the students' dormitory, but he still found it hard to sleep with the light on. He could hear the low muttering of students still working together under the light, although most were asleep by now. It was 2:00 a.m. The air smelt of stale beer and sweat and the rats kept up a constant rustling among the books and papers piled high by the dirty, uncurtained windows.

He was no nearer the solution to the problem bothering him than he had been when he had eventually put his books away and tried to sleep. Should he or should he not join the anti-government student demonstration tomorrow? His friend, Kanoni, and he had argued fiercely.

"I'm a Christian," Marcus had said. "How can I join in something I know to be against the present law of this country, and that I know will lead to violence and probably bloodshed? What will we achieve by resisting the armed forces except to get the university closed for

Requiem

the rest of the year? I want to finish my education, get my degree."

"That's a selfish point of view," Kanoni had said. "We students are the only body left in the country that still has the power to organize a demonstration, and it is our duty, as Christians, to support it. How can we let this government continue unopposed with the secret arrests, the executions, the fear and the injustices? By saying nothing we are a party to it all."

"But the Bible says that all authority comes from God," Marcus had argued, "even the bad governments. Jesus never tried to overthrow the Roman government."

"Jesus had His work to do on earth and He did it. Our work is to apply His principles to the society in which we live, and that means to strive for the freedom of man's soul and body, and for a fair and just Christian government for our country!"

And so it had gone on. Marcus turned over again, his arm across his eyes to shield them from the naked light bulb. What to do? How he wished he had been a student five years ago when the country had been quieter; when the students had been able to work and receive their degrees normally. Had that been so, he would have been where Peter, his elder brother, was now: studying in the States, safe for the moment from the violence and insecurity of their own troubled country. But it was too late to leave now. One of the first things the new military government had done was to close the borders and refuse to let people leave.

He was hot. No air circulated in the crowded dormitory. He decided to go outside for air and got up, knotting a towel around his waist. Passing through the outer wash-room, he found a group of students busy painting placards. It was the kind of thing they had to do late at night or they would have been in prison before they had a chance to display them. He stopped and read one or two that were propped up against the drab stone wall:

WHERE IS THE PROMISED PEOPLE'S GOVERNMENT?

IS THIS FREEDOM?

FREE THE POLITICAL PRISONERS!

LET THE PEOPLE SPEAK!

One of the group, a young man called Luhari, who came from Marcus's home district, glanced over his shoulder and saw Marcus watching them. He was several years older than Marcus. He put his pot of paint down for a moment and came over to him.

"Worried, Marcus?" he said kindly.

"Well...I can't sleep," confessed Marcus.

Luhari nodded. "Life would have been simpler for us if we had stayed herding cattle in our village," he said. "I can find it in myself to envy our cousins sleeping on their pile of skins in their huts. Are you worrying about tomorrow?"

"A...a little. I don't know if it's right to join in or not."

"I wondered if that would be a problem to you. You're one of these religious types, aren't you?"

Marcus flushed. "I'm a Christian, if that's what you mean," he said a little stiffly.

"So do you want an anti-religious dictatorship in your country?" Luhari asked him. "Can you not fight for your faith, if not for political reasons?"

"But it'll mean violence...bloodshed. I know you have weapons...."

Requiem

"Shhh!" Luhari gripped his arm fiercely and pulled him farther away from the others into the deeper shadow. "Don't talk so casually about such things: even here! Listen to me, Marcus...." He paused for a moment. In later days that conversation would come back to Marcus: the feel of the cold stone floor against his naked feet, the shadows cast by the flickering oil lamps, the murmur of the plotting students, and the grip of Luhari's hand as the older boy's handsome face drew near his own.

"Our country is on the verge of being a police state; you know that, don't you? Our borders are closed, our leaders are puppets in the hands of others, our old traditions a laughing-stock. If we are silent now, we will never get to speak freely again. You and I want to resist dictatorship for different reasons, I know: you, because it promises an atheistic government, and I for the sake of individual freedom, but I tell you that tomorrow will be the last chance we will have of making our voice heard in the world outside this country. There are still a few foreigners here who will see and report tomorrow's parade. We have to be heard. If this demonstration is reported in the world press, our countrymen in exile will hear it and know there are those here who would support an uprising against the present rulers. It will encourage them to return...to take back the country. If we die in this attempt...there are worse ways to die."

"But surely you do not want to return to the ways of the old nobility," Marcus said. "Was that any better than this?"

"No. But there are men abroad who are honest, right-thinking men who have the power to establish a people's government without trying to enslave men's deeds and thoughts."

Requiem

"It is a dangerous thought," Marcus said. "How do you know you are not already betrayed?"

"We are not betrayed," Luhari said, and Marcus suddenly shivered. Luhari let him go. "Go and sleep," he said. "You will need strength tomorrow." He left him and went back to the others.

Marcus went back to his bunk and fell on it, suddenly tired out. He slept.

Morning came. The placards of last night had disappeared when Marcus went through the wash-room. In the canteen, where Marcus went for breakfast, the students were for the most part silent. An uneasy calm lay over the normally noisy room. Marcus saw the servers glancing at each other. A tall, immaculately dressed student sat down at Marcus's table.

"Talk, fools!" he growled. "Do you want the whole place to be alerted?"

Thus ordered, the students began to chat among themselves. Some told a few jokes and Marcus found himself laughing; the atmosphere became more normal. Marcus was next to the student who had spoken.

"When...?" he asked timidly. "When...?"

The man did not look at him but answered, "You will know when the time comes."

Marcus went back to the dormitory to collect his books. He met Luhari there. In the daylight, his face was drawn and tired. He stopped.

"Marcus, if you are arrested, don't give your real name," he said. "They will use you to get at your brother." He made to pass on but turned back again for a moment. "Keep well to the center of the group," he said. "We have formed a band of protectors who are

Requiem

armed to surround the main body of students and keep the police off as long as possible.'

"But...the tear gas...." Marcus said, for he had seen the effect of tear gas on tightly-packed groups.

Luhari grinned suddenly. "Don't worry too much about that. We have our own supply and we've studied the wind carefully. Good luck, Marcus." He dropped his voice. "If you make it and I don't, go back to our village and try and tell them how it was...." Before Marcus could answer, he had passed on, out into the bright sunlight. Marcus never saw him again.

Marcus went to the tall university lecture block. Groups of students were standing around in the entrance hall. Perhaps there were more than usual, but it looked normal enough. In the Physics lecture there were only half the students present and the lecturer looked around, surprised.

"Where is everyone?" he asked. There was no reply and his eyes, moving from face to face, gave him the answer. He looked suddenly very tired and old. "You haven't a chance," he said in a low voice. "You know that, don't you?"

One of the students stood up.

"Please begin the lecture, sir," he said, and the lecturer walked heavily to the blackboard.

At a few minutes after nine, there was a burst of automatic fire.

"That's it," shouted the student who had spoken before. "Quickly."

They raced down the stone staircase calling encouragement to each other, leaving the teacher sitting, his head on his arms, in the empty classroom. The first part

Requiem

of the procession was already leaving the gates. On either side of the students on foot were trucks from which armed students were already firing. A wildly excited student whom Marcus knew thrust a placard into his hand.

"Here; this should suit you!" he said, and rushed on. Marcus looked up at the words painted on the wooden board:

MY COUNTRY
FOR CHRIST AND LIBERTY.

He took a firm grip and prayed fiercely beneath his breath, "Lord, I do this for You: as Your follower. If I am wrong, forgive me. If I am right, protect me." Then he was caught up in the surge of students.

In a few of the newspapers in the West the next morning, those who were interested enough to read the smaller paragraphs in the overseas section read as follows:

> The University of Nemoran has been closed for the rest of the year, following yesterday's student demonstration against the present military government.
>
> Bearing placards, the chanting students marched to one of the main crossroads of Nemoran, where a battle with police ensued. It is reported that tear gas and firearms were used by both demonstrators and police, and order was restored only by the intervention of troops.
>
> Several policemen and as many as fifty students are said to have been killed or seriously injured. A number are being held for questioning.

Requiem

In the chaos of the world news, it was insignificant enough.

In Ohio State University, in the tiny living-room of a shared student apartment, a dark-skinned, slender young scientist read the paragraphs carefully. His roommate looked over his shoulder to see what had caught his attention.

"That's where you come from, isn't it, Peter?" he said. "Sounds quite a lively affair."

"It sounds quite a serious one." Peter Nkondi put the paper down, his eyes clouded.

"Didn't you say you had a kid brother at university there?" his friend asked him.

"Yes: Marcus. I was wondering if he was in this. I hope they haven't arrested him. They could easily use him as a lever to force me back into the country."

"Force you back into the country?" Jeff Armstrong echoed his words in surprise. "Why should they need to do that? You'll go back when you've got your doctorate, won't you?"

The African looked at his young American roommate with affection. "You'll never understand, Jeff," he said. "Since the revolution my country is afraid of those of us abroad, fearing we may unite to plan rebellion while we are out of their control. They would be glad to use any means to exercise control over us…to get us back where they can dominate and rule us."

"Could you plan rebellion from here?" Jeff said curiously.

"It is not impossible," Peter said quietly.

Requiem

The cell was incredibly crowded and very cold. It smelt abominable since the only effort at sanitation was a bucket in the corner, already, after the long night, overflowing and slopping on the cement floor.

Marcus could not stop shivering. His body was a mass of bruises, many of them inflicted by the other prisoners when he, and five other students, had been flung yesterday afternoon into a cell already inhabited by too many others. The others were prisoners of all types…in there for drunkenness, theft, crimes of violence.

"Well now!" they had demanded. "You boys come from good families. What about some cell money…and quickly!"

"Cell money" was the money traditionally demanded from new prisoners under threat of a beating. Three of the students had been carrying some money and had had it snatched from them and then been left alone. Marcus and two others had nothing.

"Well," sneered the man who seemed to be the other prisoners' spokesman, "tomorrow just you get your friends and relatives to bring you some, and in the meantime we'll give you just a taste of what happens to those who forget this little courtesy," and he had hit Marcus in the mouth.

Reeling back, Marcus was kicked by those behind him and for a few minutes he felt himself kicked and beaten, lurching about helplessly in the confined space. In the end they left him, bruised and sick, to crouch against the slimy wall, retching and crying with pain. His coat had been wrenched off and all he had was his

Requiem

shirt and trousers, badly torn. His shoes had been taken by the police before he was put in the cell.

They were called out sometime during the morning—no-one still had a watch—and ordered into the interrogation room. Marcus, limping painfully and blinking at the sunlight, wondered if his ankle could be broken. They were lined up before a police captain, a sergeant snarling at them to stand straight with their heads up.

One by one they gave their names. Marcus, mindful of Luhari's warning, gave a false name. Age, course and year at the university were listed, and a photograph taken of each student. The police captain said, without much interest, "I presume most of you have given a false name. These photographs will be checked in the university records department so that you are identified correctly. There will be a penalty for those who have given false information. Line them up outside, please, Sergeant."

They were lined up in the court-yard with other students. The sergeant looked them over.

"You look a nice lot!" he said with satisfaction. "Roughed you up a bit in the cells, did they? That'll teach you to behave like fools and traitors!"

No student replied. No-one in their senses tried back-chat in a police station.

The police captain came out of the office.

"Line them up facing the wall," he said curtly. "They can stand there until the van comes to take them to prison."

With a lot of unnecessary kicks and blows the group of students, now about twenty in number, were turned to face the wall of the compound and ordered to stand

Requiem

to attention. They stood like that for five hours. Marcus felt faint with hunger and thirst as the sun rose in the sky. He had eaten nothing since the bread of yesterday's breakfast. Was it only yesterday? It seemed a week ago! But he stayed on his feet. One of the boys who, like him, had been badly beaten up in the night, fell to his knees after an hour or two. The police standing around the compound seemed to enjoy the business of kicking him to his feet again. He stood there beside Marcus, swaying, but uttering no word of complaint. Marcus felt proud that not one of the group had cried out or complained. They stood as steadily as they could, facing the wall, each one wrapped up in his own thoughts. Marcus began to pray.

Prison was, in many ways, better than the cells had been, although they had to undergo the immediate indignity of having their heads shaved. But at least the students could band together and defend themselves against the other prisoners. For the first time, Marcus heard how the demonstration had gone, and that it had been reported in the world news abroad as they had hoped. He learnt that Luhari had been killed by a policeman's club and that Kanoni had escaped.

There were other Christians in prison, too, and they had a Bible between them, which they had been allowed to keep. All the prisoners slept on a mud floor, but it was reasonably dry and they shared a thin blanket between two of them. At first the food was nearly uneatable: dried beans and hard, dry bread with sour water; but after the first week they were allowed to receive food from visitors, and Christians in the city brought them fruit and good food, which they shared. Marcus, afraid

Requiem

for his brother, had not tried to contact any relative; he had only a distant cousin in the city anyway. His ankle, bound firmly by a medical student, seemed to be healing.

During the second week of his imprisonment, he was called for interrogation and questioned about his relationship to Peter, but Nkondi was a common name and he steadfastly denied a close relationship. Eventually his cousin was brought in, and identified him as Peter's brother. Marcus was strapped to a table and beaten to punish him for telling lies. Thrown back among his friends, he was cared for tenderly but remained frightened for Peter. Days passed with no further action and no word of trial or release.

Meanwhile, in Ohio State University, Peter Nkondi was standing silently, staring at the letter that had arrived through the post. Although he had been prepared for it, it made the blood rush to his face. It was politely, even humbly, worded: an invitation to return within a month to his own country, who "had need of all her people at this time." It said, in language only slightly veiled, that unless he did so, Marcus would be shot for conspiring to overthrow the government.

So Marcus was in prison! Peter sat down at his desk, staring out at the falling leaves of autumn in the courtyard outside. He knew the prison; what man of his country did not? It was a place of filth, brutality, degradation; and Marcus was there, his sensitive and affectionate brother, who had seemed more like a son to

Requiem

him. What had made Marcus join such a demonstration? Could he abandon him, let him die?

Jeff came in whistling but stopped when he saw Peter's face.

"Something wrong?" he asked. "Bad news from home?"

Peter gestured to the letter but then realized it would mean nothing to Jeff, being in his own language.

"They have recognized my brother," he said shortly. "Unless I return, they'll shoot him."

Jeff was silent. This was beyond his experience, suggesting evil craft and deeds that had not yet touched his life. Peter looked up at him.

"You don't say 'Go,'" he said.

"What would happen to you if you did?"

"I don't know," Peter said slowly. "Maybe they would honor their word and let Marcus go free, and maybe they would simply ask me to work in a government laboratory, but in fact I think it more likely that I would be put in prison myself."

"Why should they put you in prison?" Jeff said amazed.

"They probably know some of the things I have written about them while I've been here," Peter said shortly. "They might think I need to be brain-washed before I am let loose on the public again."

Late into that night, Peter sat at his desk, thinking things out. He remembered Marcus running after him as a tiny little herd-boy, when he had just started school in the city, begging to come with him. Peter had persuaded his mother to let him pay for Marcus's education and he had lived frugally all through his university days to support Marcus at school. He remembered that Marcus had

Requiem

tried to explain in letters recently that he had become a Christian. Peter, a scientist from childhood, had had little time or inclination for religion, but he had been glad that Marcus had found a faith that made sense. Perhaps death to him would not mean the same as it meant to others. For Peter knew he would not return yet. There would be a time one day, but he could not now give up his research and voluntarily go back into the fear-ridden anarchy of the present government. Forces were gathering within and without the country that could see a people's government established and when the time was ripe, he would gladly return and help in the struggle and the rebuilding; but he could not go now, to be imprisoned, even shot, for having spoken against the government.

"You may write to your brother if you wish," said the Police Chief to Marcus after an interview at the prison.

"I have nothing to say to him that you would let me send," answered the boy proudly. "He will return when he feels it right."

"You have two more weeks," said the Police Chief curtly. "All ring-leaders of the student riot will be executed then."

"Have I been promoted to ring-leader?" Marcus said with a gleam of humor.

The policeman was silent.

The weeks in the prison had changed Marcus. He was thinner now and spoke more confidently, often acting as leader to the little group of Christians in the

Requiem

prison. They spent much time in prayer for their country and in witnessing to the other prisoners. Some of the group had gained release through influential relatives; some had been sentenced and removed to another part of the jail; others, like Marcus, still awaited their sentence. The students who had been known as the ring-leaders had been sentenced to death and were living apart all these weeks in a section of the jail known as "Life's end."

Sometimes the prisoners were made to work near or in the prison, and Marcus did that gladly to break the monotony of the long days. The rains had ended and the countryside around blazed into spring.

The day of execution for the others was fixed on a certain Saturday. On the Friday Marcus was called out of his cell and taken to the building where the condemned had been living. The student ring-leaders were there. Marcus knew them all by name. They were older, harder men than he.

"Why have you brought the boy here?" one of them, Yesagan, said curtly to the officer who had escorted Marcus. "He had no part in organizing the demonstration."

"He is condemned to die," said the man shortly, and left.

"Come here, boy," said a lanky young man, leaning against the wall beneath the high, barred window. "How old are you?"

"Twenty," Marcus said.

"Why are you condemned? Did you kill someone in the demonstration?"

"No."

"I know who he is," one of the others said. "He's Peter Nkondi's brother: the bio-chemist in America

Requiem

who's been writing for the *New York Times*. They've been trying to use him to get Nkondi home."

"And he hasn't come?"

"Obviously not, or the boy wouldn't be here."

Marcus felt young and awkward among these assured and cynical men, who seemed already to have become indifferent to death. They surrounded him, not unkindly.

"They'll not kill him," said one. "Why should they? It's only a bluff."

"I think they will," another said. "I've heard talk of this. They'll make an example of this boy to be a warning to those in similar positions. You can see their crude mentality in it!"

"Well, perhaps so," agreed Yesagan who had first spoken, and then, to Marcus, "Not to worry, kid. There are worse things to die for."

"I'm not afraid to die," Marcus said quietly. "I'm a Christian."

"A Christian?" someone said. "Caught up in all this? I thought all Christians were safely at home praying for others to overthrow the wicked government!"

"Simeon, you know that isn't true," Yesagan said. "There have been a number of Christians in the main prison. Come, Marcus. Perhaps God has sent you to us. Tell us how the Christian faith delivers you from fear of death."

And there, in that sordid enclosure of corrugated iron, a twenty-year-old student preached a sermon of which no record remains: the only witnesses those who, like him, stood on the brink of heaven or hell.

Requiem

Saturday dawned, a fresh, still day. Marcus, for all his brave testimony, trembled as he watched the square of barred light brighten opposite the tiny window. He couldn't be here. It was all a mistake, a nightmare, and he would wake up presently to find Kanoni snoring above him, and he would yawn and go over to the university canteen for tea before his first lecture! He could not really be here in this cold, dirty place!

He heard the crash of rifles, the jingle of keys, and stood up, silent as the others. There was no more to say. Their hands were tied roughly behind them. They were marched out into the early light of morning that strengthened as they walked. Marcus was aware of an unusual silence in which the commands and footsteps of their guards sounded loud; the prison seemed to be waiting, tense, behind the high, blind walls. Then, as they walked into the great central prison yard, surrounded on all sides by the high, windowless walls, a voice beyond the walls began to sing. It was such a strange sound in that place that for a moment, as the group of prisoners were halted, it seemed all were listening. The unknown voice was strong. The singer was singing the words of a Western hymn that had been translated into the local language. The words hung, sweet and unchallenged, on the morning air:

> Fight the good fight with all thy might;
> Christ is thy strength, and Christ thy right;
> Lay hold on life, and it shall be
> Thy joy and crown eternally.

Requiem

Run the straight race through God's good grace,
Lift up thine eyes, and seek His face;
Life with its way before thee lies;
Christ is the path and Christ the prize.

Life! Still ahead! Marcus felt the cloth bind his eyes but his brain was numb. He stood on the border of eternity waiting only the command of another to take the step forward to be there.

"Just a minute, Kanoni! I'm coming!" Martha Keane called from the back of the house where she had been supervising the packing of the kitchen things. As she hurried through the living-room to the front door she met her husband. "It's Kanoni Numonga, dear. Do you remember? The university student who came to speak to the high school Christian Union last year. I must have a word with him."

She invited the boy, who had been waiting outside, into the living-room. It was a mess of boxes. He looked strained and tired.

"I heard you were having to leave," he said dully, "and I thought I would say goodbye."

"That was nice of you," Martha said kindly. "Of course we are sorry to go. You know that, but the government has ordered us out. We have to leave by Tuesday." She waited, expecting some expression of regret, but Kanoni said nothing.

"I'm glad you're not arrested," Martha said. "But you have some friends still in prison? What about that nice lad I used to see you with sometimes: Marcus. Where is he?"

Requiem

"I don't know," Kanoni answered. "We can't find out what is happening inside the prison. They aren't allowed visitors now."

"How dreadful!" Martha was genuinely upset, but just then saw the lorry that had come for their boxes draw up outside their house. "Kanoni, forgive me, but I must go," she said. "Our luggage is due to go to the airport before eleven and I haven't quite finished packing."

"I know you are busy and I'll go." The boy stood up. "Mrs. Keane, you will pray for us, won't you? You can leave, but we have to stay and see it through. You must pray for us, for it…it looks as if we are losing the fight."

"I promise," Martha Keane said earnestly, but her husband and the lorry driver called her simultaneously and her mind went back to the boxes. The boy saw it. He sighed and went down the steps. He had never felt so alone in his life.

Chapter 2
The Yardstick

"No! I tell you again; it's impossible!" Allan Royce crashed his fist down on the table, making the empty teacups rattle on the plastic surface. "To transfer Sister Mary from Manara would be fatal; Damaris is just not capable of taking her place!" He glared round at the three other members of the Mission Area Council, his dark eyes burning in his pale face.

They regarded him in silence, somewhat embarrassed at his vehemence. At length, Peter Roxborough, grey-haired veteran missionary and chairman of the council, spoke.

"If you feel that strongly, Allan, we will have to let you have your way," he said dryly. "But you must realize that unless we do transfer Mary to Darii, the clinic there will have to close. Can you see any alternative?"

There was another long silence. Tense and frowning, Allan Royce stared down at the table.

"No," he said at last. "I can't. All I can see is the disaster it would be if Sister Damaris were left in sole charge of the nursing staff and dressers at Manara.

The Yardstick

She hasn't the ability, or the authority, to run such a hospital."

"If she hasn't by now there must be something pretty wrong with your training system." Ian Parker, a freckled Scot, who was supervisor of the Bible Schools in the area, joined the discussion. He was the youngest member of the council and liable to speak his mind. "Sister Damaris has understudied Sister Mary now for three years. We ought to be glad of the opportunity to nationalize this part of our work."

"It isn't really a question of not being trained." Allan pushed back his dark hair from his wet forehead and tried to answer patiently. It had been a long, hot afternoon. "There is something in the attitude of the people of this country to medical work that all our training does not change. To be a nurse, even a doctor, is seen often as a status symbol only; there is no real care for the patient or respect for human life, no sense that they are dealing with people...."

"But they have to start somewhere," Ian said abruptly. "We can't feel these things for them forever. We've got to let them run their hospitals in their way. It's the same thing as the question we discussed this morning about who keeps church funds. As long as the foreigner agrees to act as treasurer to the church, the national will never learn to care for money."

"Except," said Allan, an edge to his voice, "that in my work we're not dealing with money, but with human lives."

Peter intervened. "We've been over this before, I think," he said. "Let's keep to the point in hand. As I see it, three of us feel Sister Damaris should be asked to take full charge of the hospital at Manara and Sister Mary Duck be moved to Darii. Allan disagrees. Since Allan is

The Yardstick

the doctor in charge at Manara, I feel, myself, that we should not make this decision over his head. It seems as if we must make the decision to close Darii."

"Can we do that?" Ruth Chamberlain, the fourth council member, spoke. "I thought we only got permission to enter Darii on condition we kept the clinic staffed."

"We'll worry about that when we're sure it's the right thing to do," Peter answered. "Allan, have you anything else to say?"

Allan got up abruptly and went to the window, trying to calm the intensity of his feelings. He knew himself to be tired and over-strained and was trying to make allowance for that. He thought about the busy clinic at Darii, that mountainous little Muslim stronghold, that for years they had prayed for permission to enter; where disease held the people in its grip as surely as Allah held their souls. How could he cause it to be closed? He looked out at quiet hills now darkening to evening. Behind him, the other three awaited his decision.

"If it is truly a choice between closing Darii or moving Sister Mary," he said finally, coming back to the table, "I can't say 'close Darii.' But I still think the decision will be a disaster for Manara." He looked down at Peter closing his file. "You fraud!" he thought. "You knew all along I'd be driven into this decision. You just draw the line and wait for us to get behind it."

Peter must have read his mind, because when the meeting broke up and the clatter of dishes in the kitchen indicated that supper was being prepared, Allan found his arm taken in a friendly grip, and Peter said in his ear, "Sometimes, Allan, there is no 'right' and

The Yardstick

'wrong': only what seems to be a choice between the bad and the worse. We can only accept that God has put us into the position of having to make the choice and do the best we can."

Allan gave him a reluctant smile. "It's OK, Peter," he said. "I know it's the only thing to do; it's just that I hate to drop my medical standards."

Peter let him go. They stood in the house doorway, watching the men plod by with their oxen after the day's plowing.

"I think we must distinguish between moral principles, and standards that the West has set," Peter said. "Principles we can and must teach, but standards we can only demonstrate and then leave it to the people to decide whether or not they will accept them. Nor should we think that our standards are necessarily the right ones."

"I agree." Ruth had come up behind them to call them to supper. "I remember the kind of standards I had when I first started work at the mission office here. I was going to check stocks regularly, note each telephone call, have a system of clocking in. I wanted it to run like a good business office in England."

"And what happened?" asked Allan. "I haven't been in the mission office for some time."

Ruth laughed. "Well, it's not like that," she said. "I gave it up. There isn't another office in the city run like that. The workers thought my constant checking of stocks was pure miserliness, and I can still remember their horrified astonishment when I docked someone's wages for being late!"

"But surely," Ian had joined the group, "we should teach them how to run an efficient business. It would help them to...to...." he hesitated.

The Yardstick

"Well?" Ruth said. "Help them to do what? Do the work more quickly? If they do the work more quickly they'll need fewer men. With the present state of unemployment anything that will take jobs away from people cannot be called good. It is surely better for the country to employ more men at a lower wage than fewer men at a higher one."

"But there's the question of honesty," Ian protested. "They need to see that as important, and things like loyalty to their employer."

"Honesty in big things, yes," Ruth answered. "But we simply make no rule about the smaller things. I've come to think of it as being like picking up the last gleanings from the harvest which the Bible tells us to leave for the 'poor and the sojourners.' To concern ourselves with the small details, as we might in England, is just not worth the ill-feeling it causes."

Allan gave a short laugh. "What you're really saying," he said, "is that a sloppy, but happy, office is better than an efficient, up-tight one. Well, maybe that's what I'll have to accept at Manara, and trade my well-run, sterile hospital for a happy-go-lucky bedlam. It's just tough if you're one of those people who happen to care about their work."

He said it lightly, but there was an edge of bitterness to his tone.

The hospital at Manara had some forty beds and a large out-patient department. Allan was usually the only doctor, although from time to time young volunteer doctors would be assigned to the hospital. However, since the Mission had its own training school for nurses and dressers at Manara, there was a full staff of nurses and ancillary workers, which had been under the

The Yardstick

control of Sister Mary Duck. The patients came from a vast country area, their ailments varying from typhoid to leprosy.

Sister Damaris, now to be nurse-in-charge, was of good family and had done her training through the Mission. She had been assigned to Manara because her husband, an assistant to the provincial governor, was working in the area. She was lightly-built, somewhat nervous and quick in manner, and spoke excellent English.

During the first weeks after Sister Mary had departed in a flurry of instructions, worried notes, and over-flowing suitcases, Allan noticed very little difference. The hospital, which had been well-organized, ran for a while on the smooth wheels of the previous routine, and Allan went out of his way to show confidence in Sister Damaris, telling himself that it would not be his fault if things went wrong.

After a few weeks, he was aware that the hospital was not as clean as it used to be. The floors were not swept so often and the wards seemed dingy. He realized that some of the patients' relatives had reverted to the old practice of sleeping under their sick relation's bed. Often one or two of the hospital blankets found their way down to the floor, and once he found a severe case of pneumonia sleeping on the cold, stone floor, while husband and sister shared the bed above. He had complained about that one, but shut his lips on the rest while he was trying to work out in his mind the difference between a moral principle and a non-essential Western "standard."

Then he noticed that the nurses had begun to wear cardigans over their uniforms. Being a man, he took some time to become aware of this, but, since the

The Yardstick

cardigans were usually old, of any color and frequently dirty, he eventually took notice. In the operating theatre he once saw the sleeve of a filthy cardigan falling beneath the operating-gown sleeve and sharply ordered the nurse to go and take it off. When the woman they were delivering, a particularly awkward forceps delivery, was back in a few days with an infected uterus, Allan sent for the girl and told her off. Later, Sister Damaris said, "I hear you rebuked Nurse Rahel, Doctor Royce. I really think it is my work to speak to the nurses about their faults."

"Then I suggest you stop them wearing these filthy cardigans over their uniforms!" Allan snapped, tired after a difficult operation.

"The girls complain of being cold," Sister Damaris said. "I cannot very well insist they do not dress warmly enough."

Allan, with a tremendous effort of will, said nothing more.

"It isn't only those wretched cardigans!" he fumed to a young volunteer doctor, David Hill, who had come to spend a few months with him. "It's the dirty uniforms, the smelly toilets, the filthy floors. Do you know, yesterday I had to tell someone to clean mud off the operating room floor before I started the operation? Just think how great it would be to slip with a scalpel in your hand just when you're going to slit someone's belly open!"

"Why don't you just have a show-down with her?" David suggested. "Perhaps all she needs is a reminder."

"She needs more than that!" growled Allan. "All the telling in the world isn't going to change her into a different person, and I don't want to make more barriers between us than there are already. Anyway,

The Yardstick

it's true that it's not really my business to correct her staff."

On his rounds the next day Allan, who had Sister Damaris and David with him, stopped short in the doorway of a room he had not been intending to enter, to see one of the hospital orderlies working on setting up a drip. He seemed to be jabbing ineffectually at the patient's arm. He entered the room.

"What are you doing?" he said curtly.

"Oh, good-morning, Doctor," the orderly said cheerfully. "I was just getting this drip going again. It slipped out last night and there wasn't anyone around to put it back."

Allan turned to Sister Damaris. "Where are the dressers? Surely there is always one of them on duty in this ward?"

"They asked to attend a funeral," Sister Damaris said reluctantly.

"All of them?"

"Yes. It was Ginja's brother."

"So they go off to sit doing nothing in a tent, while an orderly does their work for them?" said Allen incredulously.

Sister Damaris bit her lip. "I did not know this drip was not functioning correctly, Doctor," she said stiffly. "I will see to it myself," and she moved forward.

"Oh, don't worry, Sister," the orderly said cheerfully. "I often do it for them without trouble. It's just that this chap's arm was on the thin side and I couldn't get the right vein straight away."

"Come, Doctor Hill," said Allan tensely to David, and swung out of the room.

The Yardstick

David, following him to the ward they had been going to, wisely made no comment. They continued their round more or less in silence. Sister Damaris joined them shortly. Allan said to her, "I'm ready to start operating now, Sister. Who is going to act as anesthetist? Another orderly?"

"I will assign a nurse to you immediately," Sister Damaris said. "I am sorry the dressers are absent. I didn't approve of their going but they made it very difficult for me to stop them."

"You are in charge of them," Allan said, trying to speak normally. "Couldn't you have reminded them that they have some responsibility for the patients in their wards?"

"They saw their greatest responsibility as being to Ginja's family," replied Damaris. "I did my best."

Later that morning, David was taking out patients when Allan put his head round the door.

"David, my nurse anesthetist has just taken her child for an injection," he said. "I am about to do an urgent appendectomy. Would you be so kind as to come and act as anesthetist?"

"But...." David began. Allan came right into the room.

"For heaven's sake, David, come!" he said sharply. "Apparently there's no-one else I can insist obeys me. You, at least, are under my authority!"

David saw that the older man was holding his temper in check with difficulty, shrugged, and said to the nurse with him. "Deal with what you can. Tell the rest to come back tomorrow," and followed Allan to the operating theatre.

The Yardstick

An hour or two later, when they were stripping off their gowns, Allan said, "Sorry I took you from out-patients, David, but honestly, I'd had all I could stand."

"It's OK," David pulled the cap off and shook out his fair hair. "Did the nurse just announce she was leaving?"

"She said Sister Damaris had given her permission to go yesterday."

"Well…Damaris wouldn't have known the dressers were going to take off, yesterday," David said.

"I suppose not." Allan made an effort to calm himself down. "But how this hospital is going to continue like this, I don't know!"

"Do you want me to talk to Mr. Roxborough about it when I go back to headquarters next month?" asked David, but Allan shook his head.

"No, I'm getting through this one myself. The Lord has the answer somewhere. I'll just keep praying."

"I wondered when you were going to say that," David said. "I thought you missionaries always did things that way."

"We do." Allan grinned, rather shamefacedly. "But maybe we don't shout about it that much. I know God will do something; change me, change Damaris, even change the hospital so that we can be seen to live together as Christians in a place that belongs to Him."

At first sight, the woman was as all other women: sitting quietly in out-patients, holding her baby wrapped in a dirty shawl. Allan unwrapped the child and laid him on the table. The mother spoke, softly and

The Yardstick

intensely, in the local dialect, "Doctor, please, the baby must live."

He glanced down at her, his attention caught by the beautiful but frantic eyes.

"We will do our best for him," he said gently.

"More than that. Pray to your god. He must live! He must! I will pay anything, anything!"

"It isn't a question of money," Allan said, examining the child, who obviously had been suffering from severe dysentery for some days and was very dehydrated. "How long has he been like this?"

"Many days," the woman said. "We tried all we knew and now have been walking for two days to reach here. We are from the border country."

"Is your husband with you?" Allan asked.

"No. He was away. The child must be cured before he returns. You see I have only given him dead children; this one only lived. If he dies my husband will divorce me, find another wife who can give him children. On this child is my life."

The speech was muttered, with hanging head, but Allan knew she spoke the truth. In her tribe it was hard indeed for a wife who could not bear children.

"We will try," he said. "The child must stay here in hospital, but you may stay with him."

The woman knelt to kiss his feet and he suffered it in silence.

The child was very sick. With some difficulty Allan himself put up a subcutaneous drip, and wrote down an order for hourly feeds by mouth. It was evening, so he filled in the form for night instructions and asked which nurse was on duty.

The Yardstick

"It is Nurse Rahel, Doctor," Sister Damaris said. "I will mention it to her particularly."

"Very good," Allan said, busily writing up another drug.

He checked the child at seven, before he went off for the night. David, knowing of his interest in the case, came with him. They looked at the child together.

"I think he'll make it," said Allan, pleased at the response and seeing the temperature was beginning to fall. The tiny chest was rising and falling rhythmically and the breathing was much less labored. He smiled and nodded at the woman who stood there with an older woman, perhaps her mother, beside her, and said curtly to Rahel as he passed, "Watch the child, Nurse, and let me know at once if there is any change." Then he went off and flung himself wearily down in his bachelor sitting-room with relief.

He was awakened in the night by the sound of wailing. There was nothing especially unusual in hearing that sad sound in hospital, but, as full consciousness returned, Allan sat up with a jerk. What patient was near death in the hospital? Surely only the child. The child! How could he have died? Perhaps it was a new patient brought in, and discovered to be dead on arrival. Allan fumbled for his torch to look at the time: 2:20 AM. Who traveled through the African bush at two in the morning? He began to get out of bed and so was prepared for David, who came in with a flashlight.

"They want you at the hospital," David said flatly. "A messenger has just come."

Allan fumbled around for his shoes. "But why?" he said, "What is it?"

"The child is dead."

The Yardstick

In the cold, dark hospital a pressure lamp was burning over the bed on which the child lay. A group of wailing women clustered around the door of the ward. Allan pushed through them and stared unbelievingly at the child. Its tiny body was quite still, the skin taut over its bones, its eyes sunken and staring in the head which looked far too large for the rest of the body. It was obviously dead.

Allan caught up the board of medical treatment, half-expecting what he would find. The child had not been fed since nine o'clock the previous evening. Allan felt the blood rush to his head. He turned to the trainee dresser who was holding the lamp.

"Where is Nurse Rahel?"

"She went off...some time ago. She said a relative was ill."

"She ignored these night instructions, just went without a word?"

The dresser was aware of the doctor's rising anger and answered reluctantly. "She said I had to watch that the drip did not come out."

"But the hourly feeds? What of them?"

"She didn't say anything about feeds."

Allan swung around. "Get Sister Damaris."

"Doctor...she's in bed."

"Well, get her out of it!"

David, at Allan's side, intervened. "Allan, please, not now. The child is dead. Talk it over in the morning. Don't have a scene now: in the middle of the night and when you're so angry."

Allan paused. It was the voice of reason.

"It is only a poor woman from the border country," the dresser muttered sullenly. "Why do we make such a fuss over one baby?"

The Yardstick

"One baby," Allan repeated in a low tense voice that trembled with rage. "One life: one immortal soul that had as much right to live as you or I, one creature formed in the image of God! You see it as less important than the death of a cow, don't you?"

There was a second's silence and then renewed wailing rose at the door. A man ran in. "The mother! She has tried to hang herself from the tree outside."

They carried her in and laid her beside the body of her child. Her throat was bruised and cut where the rope had been, her tongue forced out between her lips. She was breathing stertorously. Allan looked down at her in pity, remembering her words, "On this child is my life" and his rage at the needless death rose again. David spoke at his elbow.

"Why don't you let me see to her, Allan? She doesn't seem too badly hurt. Go back to the house."

When David came in, forty minutes later, he found Allan, burning-eyed, slumped into a chair, a candle alight beside him.

"Well?" he said thickly. "How is she?"

"She'll live," David said shortly. "Can I make some coffee?"

"It's at times like this," Allan said, watching David get the cups out, "that I wish I drank something stronger than coffee! I'd like to drink myself into insensibility. Live! I expect she only wants to die!"

"It happens," said David. "Surely this isn't the first time you've lost a patient that you hoped to save?"

"No, it isn't," Allan said hoarsely. "But I usually lose them because of ignorance, because the relatives didn't know any better, or because they bring them in too late, or they are too sick for me to help them anyway. This is

The Yardstick

the first death I've seen through sheer negligence: because a nurse wanted to go off duty." He got up, lurching unsteadily to the kitchen, where David stood over the primus. "I can tell you one thing, though," he said. "It won't be the last. They don't care here, and nothing I can do will make them care. Life. Death. It is 'the will of God': and I have to stand by and watch murder done and do nothing except say, 'Oh dear! Did someone forget?'"

David poured out the coffee.

"Maybe it is we who have the wrong idea," he said. "We, who prolong our lives to the last gasp, and hook up to machines when the body gives way. Maybe we have got it wrong."

"No." Allan took the cup and sat down again. "No. We are not animals. There is something worth fighting for in the human life...even in the life of one little African baby."

David took his cup and sat down, and after a moment Allan said, "Where did you put the mother? In the same bed?"

"No, Sister Damaris came and took her to her own home," David answered. "She was so depressed they thought she might try it again if she was left in the ward."

"So Sister Damaris turned up, did she?" Allan said without expression. "Tell me, did Nurse Rahel arrive on the scene?"

"No, but I know one thing," David said. "Damaris didn't know Rahel was intending to leave the hospital tonight. It certainly wasn't with permission."

"Dear me. I hope she tells her what a naughty girl she is." Allan suddenly stood up. "I'd better get off to

The Yardstick

bed, David, before I get as catty as a woman," he said. "I'm sorry. I'll be fine in the morning."

Allan avoided Sister Damaris in the morning, but at noon she approached him in a ward.

"Doctor, could I see you for a moment?" she asked stiffly.

He could not well refuse and followed her reluctantly into her office. They looked at each other. To his amazement, there were suddenly tears in her eyes.

"I wanted to say," she said unsteadily, "that I accept responsibility for that baby's death, and I'm sorry."

It meant a lot for a national to say that honestly to a white man, and Allan stared at her. "You...minded?" he said incredulously.

She flushed. "Very, very much," she said and sat down at her desk. He came and stood in front of her, looking down at her. "I knew you thought this sort of thing didn't matter to me," she went on slowly. "I know you have been comparing me always with Sister Mary, and that you've missed her. So have I—very much. You see it's all right for you missionaries to give orders and expect them to be obeyed, to tell us to keep things clean, to come on time, to work stated hours; it's part of your culture and we accept it. But this kind of thing isn't part of our culture and it is hard for me to give similar orders when they know and I know that it is unnatural for us to treat people in that way."

"I know that in part," Allan said. "I'm sorry if you thought I was always criticizing. I have tried to be understanding and not interfere."

"But I knew what you thought," Damaris smiled wryly. "Every time you frowned at dirt on the floor, or were kept waiting for someone, or didn't have the

The Yardstick

equipment you needed, I knew it. These things..." she hesitated.

"Go on," said Allan.

"These things are so important to you, but we have to decide for ourselves whether they're important to us or not," Damaris said slowly, "and maybe there's something in our way of life that is different, even better than yours. But other things, things that are necessary to save life, those things are important to us both. I have dismissed Nurse Rahel."

"Dismissed her?" Allan was startled.

"Yes. Her relative was not greatly sick, and she said to me, 'Why does it matter so much? It was only a poor woman's baby.'"

"And that made you angry?" Allan said hungrily.

"Very angry," Sister Damaris said. "That is one thing I have learnt from you and Sister Mary, one thing I believe in and will live by: the dignity, the importance of human life. Any human life."

Allan smiled and stretched out his hand.

"If we start there, Sister," he said, "we're starting on the right road!"

She took his hand.

Chapter 3
The Strike

Bill Underwood, Director of the Mission Language School, stood at his study window, watching a little scene outside. One of the language-school students, Greta, from Sweden, was holding out a towel to the African girl who did the washing, and saying politely, "Have you begun the wash, Esther? Please add this. I forgot it."

Esther frowned. "I have enough washing!" she said sharply. "You no add more."

The Swedish girl, who had been only a few weeks in Africa, was uncertain how to react.

"But only one towel...." she began.

"Five towels now!" the girl answered sulkily, making no move to take the one the missionary recruit was still holding out to her.

Bill saw Greta struggle within herself and was sorry that what she obviously considered her "better self" won.

"All right, Esther. I'll wash it myself," she said and went off, a picture of Christian meekness.

The Strike

Bill went back to his desk. Greta's prayer-letter, written to her supporters at home, lay on it. He usually suggested, though never insisted, that his students let him read the circular letters that they sent out to their prayer supporters: really to avoid any unwise remarks in them that might offend the very sensitive government under which they lived. Greta, an extremely conscientious student, had provided him with an English translation of her Swedish letter. He picked it up and read:

"Of course, almost the first people we meet are the young African girls who help us in the house. The one who works for me is called Esther, a sweet girl. She is not a Christian yet, but I feel sure that if you pray for her, she will believe soon. I have had several long talks with her because she understands English quite well, and yesterday was showing her all of your photographs and telling her about my church in Sweden who would pray for her. We had tea together. How strange it felt to be sitting drinking tea with one from this land at last! I hope she will be my first friend."

And all that, Bill reflected cynically, was probably the trouble with Esther now. One day Greta would learn how to treat her servant in a way that led to a happy and healthy relationship. Meanwhile—as a knock came on the door—he had his own troubles to deal with.

He sat down at his desk: a burly, sun-burnt man with crisp, greying hair, exuding a confidence and authority he did not always feel, and said in the national language, "Come in!"

Ledda, who came in, was a tall, young African who would have been handsome had it not been for his permanently sullen expression. He was dressed neatly in a white polo-necked jersey and dark trousers. Although he came in aggressively, even angrily, his people's innate

The Strike

politeness still had him in its grip. He bowed his head and took Bill's out-stretched hand, the words of greeting coming automatically to his lips:

"May God give you happiness forever."

"And to you and yours."

"It is only in our culture," thought Bill fleetingly, "that a man ignores the need of a greeting when he is angry or annoyed." He remembered an American student coming in only that morning with the words, "Now, see here, Bill...." on his lips. But, such as they were, the greetings were now over. Ledda had sat down and was looking defiantly at him. He cleared his throat.

"I've read your letter, Ledda," he said. "It seems the three main demands in it are the dismissal of my wife as a teacher in the school, a general increase in pay for all teachers and informants, and also free housing for you and your families. The other things are smaller issues and we can deal with them later.'

"Very well," the young man answered. "Let us discuss those three."

"Then tell me what you have against my wife as a teacher."

"She has interfered with our marking of the term tests," said Ledda. "Several times she has lowered the marks we give, without reason. Just because she is a bad teacher and her students do not do well, there is no reason why we should give our students bad marks."

Bill had been prepared for this.

"It was I who changed the test markings for the first-year students," he said.

"Because of what she said."

"Because of the evidence of my own eyes," said Bill, refusing to let his voice change from its normal even tone. He took a paper from a drawer and put it in front

The Strike

of Ledda. "Study this, Ledda. The red marks are the markings of Joseph. I myself corrected the exercise afterwards in green. Many of the mistakes had not been corrected at all. It is not fair to give this back to the student with a mark of ninety-eight per cent on it." The paper had far more green marks on it than red.

Ledda scowled. "We are in Africa," he said. "Our custom is not to discourage the student by giving him low marks. It is better for him to think he is doing very well; then he will work better."

Bill took the paper back. "We are in Africa," he agreed, "but these students are students from my country and other Western countries. They are used to different standards. It does not help them to give them high marks, if they feel they haven't earned them, and it is not good to mark mistakes as correct."

The discussion went on. The money question, Bill knew, would be a trying one. Inwardly exasperated, he kept a tight hold on his temper.

"You teachers are getting fifty dollars more a month than your own government would pay you in a government school," he said. "Your hours are much shorter. The informants, who are not trained at all, get nearly as much. The Mission cannot afford to give you more."

"The rise in the standard of living...." began Ledda, but Bill cut him short.

"We have taken that into account continually," he said. "I know how much it costs you to live, and you can all easily live on what we give you."

"Could *you*?" asked Ledda.

"We do!" Bill said. "You get paid more than I do. Ask the mission treasurer."

"But your monthly wage doesn't represent all you get," said Ledda sullenly. "You don't pay rent, traveling

The Strike

expenses, medical fees. You have the use of cars and get free furniture and equipment. You don't need to buy clothes since you come with cheap clothes from your own country."

Not for the first time Bill regretted the fact that the language students talked so freely with the African staff about mission business. Ledda read his face.

"Yes, it is true we learn this from the students," he said. "They haven't learnt yet not to talk honestly and freely to us. They see things as they really are. You live as the rich and we as the poor. Why don't we own cars to visit the city when we wish, and buy expensive fruit and canned food?"

He paused and Bill said, "Is it any use to tell you I am over twice your age? Perhaps in twenty years time, you will have all these things and more. You know as well as I do that there are Africans in the city who live at a far higher standard than we do."

But Ledda was too worked up now to listen.

"At first when you come," he said bitterly, "you are friendly and kind. You listen sympathetically and with interest. But then you get hard. You continue to talk of love but you talk with the lips, not with the heart. You give us small wages saying that the mission is poor and has little money; but who would believe that, seeing your possessions? I am warning you; unless you raise our salaries, we will not work. We will have a strike!"

Bill looked at him and spoke quietly, "You accuse us of not being Christians because we do not give you all you want," he said. "Do you think your attitude now and threats to us are Christian in tone?"

"It is the Christianity you have taught us!" said Ledda, and got up to leave.

The Strike

Bill sat still at the desk, that last sentence ringing in his ears. His hands were clenched and, after a moment, he looked down at them and opened them, whispering, "Lord, what now? Guide us through this one." Then he realized that Diana, his wife, had come in. She put her arm around him.

"They'll calm down," she said gently. "The church elders will be able to talk to them. It won't get to the stage of a strike."

"I think it will," said Bill wearily. "But it doesn't make any difference. I can't possibly give them what they want even if they go on strike. If the mission could be forced into giving out more money by such means there'd be strikes on every mission station within a month."

"And if they do go on strike," Diana asked. "What then?"

Bill got up and went to the window.

"I suppose I'll have to phone headquarters and Ken will have to come up and settle it," he said gloomily. "After all, they only want to make us crawl a bit. Ken is a big enough person to soothe their pride. If they cause him to come up here and pour out all their complaints to him, he can probably sort it out for us."

"Poor Ken!" Diana said with feeling, knowing how harassed and over-worked the big, good-tempered Head of Mission was already. "Can't we manage without him?"

"If those wretched recruits wouldn't interfere," said Bill, suddenly angry, "we probably could. It's they who've put them up to this, you know."

He leant out of the window from where he had been watching an English boy talking earnestly with Ledda

The Strike

and some of the informants. "Hey, Barry! Barry Morton! Come over here a moment!"

The student addressed, a big, loose-limbed fellow with unruly fair hair, looked up, not very pleased at the peremptory summons. Nevertheless, he detached himself from the group and came up to the window.

"I want to talk to you," Bill said looking down at him. "Come into the office." Then he said to Diana, "Leave us alone, Darling. I won't be long."

"All right. Don't eat him, will you?" Diana smiled a little anxiously, and left the room.

"Yes?" Barry stood in the middle of the room, looking a little belligerent. Bill did not waste words.

"I take it you agree with Ledda and his friends," he said. "In fact you are one of the students who have encouraged him to make these demands?"

"Well...er...yes," Barry said, rather unprepared for this direct clash with his Principal. "I do think it's wrong that we live at such different standards and that we have so much more than they do."

"OK," Bill sat down but did not invite the boy to do so. "You must know that the Mission has difficulty in meeting our needs. Do you really think we could keep all our employees living at the same standard?"

"No." Barry was recovering, organizing his arguments. "But I don't think we should live at such a high standard. We could do with much less."

"Perhaps," Bill said. "I think I have a request form for you here?" He began to search through some forms on his desk. "Yes...here it is. You want the Volkswagen to drive Eileen into the city on Saturday for the baby's injection. Is that right?"

"Yes." Barry was mystified at the sudden change of subject.

The Strike

"Well," Bill said calmly. "Request denied."

"B...but," stuttered the boy, "we have to take him in. It's dangerous without it."

"The clinic here can give the same injection."

"But it's not the same injection...and anyway the needles here are all infected and our children have no resistance to these diseases...."

"Well then; Eileen can take the child in on the bus. That's what Ledda's wife would have to do if they wanted to go to the city."

There was a silence. The bus. Barry thought about the prospect: two days of hot, dusty travel, with a baby, and a night at a local inn with the lice and bedbugs.

The silence lengthened.

"Well?" Bill said eventually, more gently. "I've given you something to think about, haven't I?"

"Yes, Sir," Barry said soberly.

"Well, go away and think about it; and next time think your ideas through more carefully before you spread them all over the school."

Head bowed, Barry left the room and Bill, feeling a little better, went into the living-room where supper had been prepared. Diana looked at him accusingly and he grinned a little shamefacedly.

"You heard?" he said.

"The walls are only mud," Diana said defensively, and then, "You aren't going to stick to that, Bill, are you? You were a bit hard on him."

"What? Oh, you mean am I going to make Eileen go on the bus? No, of course not." Bill poured himself some coffee. "I only wanted to give him a bit of a fright...slow him down a little before he makes too much of a fool of himself. I'm afraid experience is the only teacher when it comes to living here."

The Strike

"Especially with the servants," Diana said with a sigh. "I had Greta in here just now, in tears because Esther had been so rude to her. How could I explain that she'd really been too familiar with her? It's the exact opposite to all their books on the mission-field have taught them!"

"What did you say?" Bill asked curiously.

"I suggested that she should watch to see how the African Christians treated their servants," Diana said.

"Well," Bill said doubtfully, "I suppose some of them treat them well, but many still think of them as slaves. The truth is that we aren't committed to follow the African culture any more than we are committed to our own. Our only commitment is to the biblical way of doing things."

Next day, the three African teachers and six informants went off towards the town in a sullen group at a quarter past eight. At eight-thirty Bill faced the twenty-two language students in the main classroom.

"I'm afraid we're in this together," he said to them. "Have any of you anything you want to say? I'd rather hear your point of view now than have you also split into little groups to air your opinions!"

He avoided looking too obviously at Barry Morton, but Barry was silent. Eventually a Canadian student said, "I guess we don't know enough about the problem, Bill. I'd just like to say I'm sorry you're in trouble and anything I can do to help I'd be glad to do."

There were murmurs of agreement and Bill smiled.

"Thank you," he said. "I want you to continue in class for the next two hours. Diana and I will give you

The Strike

instruction, and then we'll give you an assignment that will last for the rest of the morning. We'll have to take it a day at a time."

At the house Diana met him. "Pastor Debenko is here," she said. "He's in the living-room."

"Good," Bill said. "Will you take on the students while I talk to him? If you give the second group an exercise and teach the first, I'll take over in an hour's time if I can."

Diana nodded and went off. Bill greeted with affection the tall, black pastor with a wide, ugly mouth that could split into an attractive grin. "I hoped you'd come up, Pastor Debenko. May God give you happiness."

"And to you and yours," the pastor answered in the gentle voice, so much at variance with his huge frame.

Bill called to the girl to bring coffee, and they sat down. For a while there was silence; then Bill looked across at his friend.

"We've been friends a long time, Brother," he said. "If you want to say anything in rebuke to me, say it. If I'm making a mistake I'll gladly give in and try and put things right. Have you discussed the matter with the other elders?"

"Not yet. There has not been time," Debenko answered, blinking through his glasses as the morning sun streamed through the window. "The young men have not come to us; if they had, we would have counseled patience." He sighed. "The young of today are always dissatisfied."

The coffee came and Bill poured it out.

"Tell me, Brother," he said. "What answer can there be to this eternal problem of living standards? Does it offend you always that this house is nicer than yours?

The Strike

That we eat differently, have more books, more furniture?"

The pastor did not answer at once. He seemed to be choosing his words carefully. Then he said, "Bill, is there no-one in your country richer than you are?"

"Of course there are," Bill said. "Plenty."

"And they own more than you do? Travel more? Live in better houses?"

"Yes."

"Well...what do you feel about them? Does it worry you? Do you want to take it from them or make them give it to you?"

"Not usually," Bill said thoughtfully. "I don't know that I think that much about it, especially when I'm spiritually fit. That's just the way things are. I have enough."

"So, we have enough," the pastor said quietly. "There will always be different standards in life; why else was the tenth commandment ever written? If we gain one standard, we immediately want a higher. I don't think we would be satisfied until we were all kings." He paused and smiled. "And what we must do is realize that we all *are* kings in the spirit, and see material things as second to those of the spirit." He took off his glasses and polished them, glancing rather shyly at Bill. "And what you must do is show us that, whether you have much or little, it is second in your life to the true spiritual riches of Christ."

"It is truly spoken," said Bill soberly.

There was a silence. Then the pastor said, "We will try and talk to Ledda, but at the moment they are in one of the town bars, drinking. We must wait for a quieter moment." He got up to go. "I came to say we will help you all we can. This kind of thing is happening all over

The Strike

the country. It is the days we live in, not just you and your cars!"

At the time of the mid-morning break Bill and Diana met with the students for prayer, and then Bill took charge of the classes. He was explaining a grammatical error when something so unexpected happened that he took a moment to realize that it was happening.

There was a sudden sound of shouting outside the compound and a crash as something hit the tin gate. The next moment a stone came through the window of the classroom and landed on Bill's desk, sending splintered glass in every direction. Before he could get to his feet the door burst open and a mob from the town pushed its way into the room, shouting and waving sticks. Bill leapt to his feet and seized the wrist of the leader: a man in the dress of a laborer, with an iron bar, his breath smelling strongly of drink.

"What the devil are you doing?" he said furiously in English. "Get out of this compound!" They struggled together against the noise of over-turned furniture and women's screams. Bill, desperately anxious for Diana and what could be happening in the house, used all his strength and wrested the bar from the man. He tripped him up so that he fell sprawling, and dashed for the door yelling, "Get the women into the library!"

Most of the women students were huddling against the far wall of the classroom and seemed to be unmolested. Bill grabbed the arm of one of the heftier students, "Tim! Get the women into the library and stand guard at the door!" The library was an inner room without windows.

The young man nodded and, dodging a viciously-thrown rock, ran across the classroom, kicking furniture

The Strike

aside. Bill stopped once more to shout to another man, "Try and protect the cars!" and then made it into his house.

Diana and young Barry's wife, holding her baby, were standing helplessly in the living-room, while four or five men were laying about them with sticks, smashing up the furniture and laughing. Bill saw a heavy tape-recorder pushed over to fall splintering on the floor, and a bookcase ripped from the wall to fall forward, spilling books in every direction. He caught hold of Diana's arm and said to them both, "Quick! Into the bathroom."

He herded them into the little room and shut the door on them. One man tried to follow them. Bill lifted the iron bar he was still carrying and practically broke the upraised arm with it. The man let out a yell of pain.

"Now get out!" roared Bill, "or the next one will be on your head!"

A nearly-demented Barry hurled himself into the room.

"Eileen!" he gasped. "I can't find her!"

"It's OK. She and Diana are in the bathroom with the baby," Bill said. "Stand guard here for a moment while I hustle these men on their way."

But the noise was getting less and men were running for the gate. The compound was nearly clear except for the students, some of whom were nursing various wounds. Bill looked around at the buildings. In the classroom block every window was smashed. Rocks, broken furniture, torn books, parts of recording machines, glass, littered the ground everywhere. Silently, the students gathered.

"Is anyone badly hurt?" Bill asked looking down at them.

The Strike

"Just cuts and bruises, I think," a German boy answered, holding a cloth to his head, which was bleeding freely.

"Were you women harmed?"

"No," one answered. "They didn't come into the store-room. We shut ourselves in there."

"Come into the house," Bill said. "I suppose they are all in the same state."

He saw the servants beginning to come back into the compound. Fora, the day watchman, was wringing his hands, "Oh, Mr. Bill. How terrible this is!" he groaned. "What could I do? I could not hold the gate against them. They threatened to kill me...."

"It's all right," Bill said. "But go now, down to the police station and tell them what has happened. Ask them to send someone up here at once."

In the wrecked living-room, from which Diana was sweeping glass, the students gathered. Someone brought the first-aid boxes. The baby, silent in all the noise, was now screaming. Bill did a quick head-count and was relieved to find everyone there.

"How about the cars?" he asked.

"We fought over them," a small red-haired youth said, grinning nervously. "They're a bit dented and one windscreen has gone...but they'll go all right."

"Well, ladies, go and pack," Bill said. "We'll have to move into the city for the time being, and you can be off before nightfall. Husbands can go in the first batch, but only one suitcase each, please. Single men stay with me and we'll try and sort things out a bit."

An hour later, Bill saw the convoy off. By that time police were strolling around the compound. "Probably

The Strike

seeing what they can loot too," thought Bill, watching them.

Barry Morton came by, ready to take the wheel of the Volkswagen combi that had lost its windscreen. He paused when he saw Bill.

"Bill," he said awkwardly, "Ledda and his friends were behind this, weren't they? I hope...well, I was wondering if I had been responsible...I never thought...." his voice tailed off miserably.

Bill took pity on him. "It probably would have happened anyway, Barry," he said. "It's happening all over the country in one way or another. Don't worry about it now; we'll talk it over when we meet at headquarters."

He stuck his head into the combi. Strained, white faces looked at him. He grinned. "See you in the city," he said. "We'll sort it all out there. Don't worry on the journey. What you've just experienced is a group of drunks here in this town, not the beginnings of civil war. We'll pack up what we can save of the stuff that remains, put it under police guard, and leave the buildings to be repaired. We'll see you all in a day or two."

Five days later, Bill sat opposite the big, blond Head of Mission in the city, hating himself for adding to the load Ken Marshall was already carrying in the troubled country.

"I'm sorry it happened to recruits," Ken was saying thoughtfully. "I hope they'll get over it, but it takes time. We'll leave the place to cool off for a week or two, and then you and I will go back and see what we can do. You say you've moved the stuff worth saving into the one good building and left a police guard there, so there's

The Strike

no great hurry. I'll ask the elders to come in and see us later this week. How's that?"

"Fine." Bill stood up to go but hesitated. "Ken," he said, "do you think this was my fault? I keep wondering if I should have handled it differently, tried to pacify Ledda more. And yet how can the Mission give in to what amounts to blackmail?"

Ken leant back in his chair, looking up kindly at his worried colleague. "Bill, I believe God is in every situation," he said slowly. "He put you in charge of that language school and He knew the person you are and what was going to happen. You prayed, and did as you felt right. That's all you could do."

"But supposing I wasn't right?"

"Are you supposing that simply because things seem to have gone wrong?" asked Ken. "Things are never trouble-free for any child of God. All we can do is accept the difficulties as part of God's plan for us and trust God through them and out the other side." He smiled. "Don't look back, Bill. Start planning for the future."

"Well—actually—talking of that," Bill said, "I was thinking of getting the students together and setting up classes for the time being here in the city. It would be better for them to keep working."

"Fine." Ken got up to leave the office himself. "We'll never have all the answers, Bill, and in any case some problems just don't have answers, despite all the literature on the 'new image of mission' that is coming off the Western presses." He collected some papers and began to put them in a brief-case. "Loving people, whatever they do, whatever they say, however they hurt us; being to them the fragrance of Christ in God…that's the nearest I can get to a fool-proof formula."

Together they went out into the hard, bright sunshine.

Chapter 4
The Love-Match

Lorraine stopped the station-wagon near the top of the hill, pulling into the woods beside the road. She turned to her companion. "Let's walk for a while in the woods," she suggested.

Solomon looked around a little uneasily. "If you like," he said, "but we'd better not go too far from the car. Woods like these are not really safe. This is a well-known place for robbers."

"Oh," Lorraine said laughing. "That's what you hear us foreigners say. I'll rely on you to protect me. Aren't the people around here from your own tribe?"

But Solomon refused to take it lightly. "Never think it's only the whites who are attacked," he said. "They would not hesitate to beat me and rob me if they thought I had anything worth having: especially if they see me walking with a white girl."

Lorraine felt a familiar little stab of hurt and made no move to get out of the car. "Well then," she said good-humoredly, "let's go on somewhere else. I only wanted to be able to walk a little with you. Where shall we go? Down into the plain for a little way?"

The Love-Match

He agreed and she started the engine.

Presently they stopped again, in open land, and, locking the car, started to walk down a village track bordered by fields. Almost at once Lorraine heard the yodeling of the herd-boys and knew that in minutes the little boys would be around them: intrigued at the sight of a white girl walking with one of their own people. She turned hastily to Solomon.

"Solomon, I wanted to ask you when your father will be in town," she said. "Surely it is time I met him."

"Darling, don't be so impatient," Solomon said, taking her hand. "I've got to explain it to my parents slowly. I told you that."

"But do your people so dislike the idea of your marrying a foreigner?" Lorraine said. "Why did you say, up there in the wood, that you would be more likely to be attacked when I was with you?"

"It is only because they are ignorant and uneducated," Solomon said, frowning a little. "In the towns so many people do it that it is no problem. Anyway, in the Christian church we are all meant to be one in Christ; so Christians cannot object to it."

"But with the country dwellers?" Lorraine asked. "Will there always be difficulties with them? When we're married, I want to be one of your people. Will they always think of me as a foreigner?"

As if in mocking echo of her words, little boys now near them shouted, "Foreigner! Foreigner!"

With an angry exclamation, Solomon let go Lorraine's hand and turned on the children with a torrent of angry words. When they retorted, he stooped, pretending to pick up stones.

The Love-Match

"Ah don't!" Lorraine laid her hand on his arm and spoke gently to the children, but, although they paused in their flight, they stared at her uncomprehendingly.

"They are tribes children," Solomon said. "They won't understand the city language. Come, let us go back to the car."

They turned back, walking apart, but Solomon went on talking, for they were speaking in English and none of the children would be able to understand.

"Lorraine, don't doubt me," he was saying gently. "When I feel the time is right, I will take you to my family. I will present you to them as my intended wife and they will not be able to reject you."

"But will they want to?" Lorraine thought, her eyes on the distant hills that bordered the dusty plain they were in. There was something else she wanted to say before they got back to the town.

"Solomon," she said. "When we get married...I want to be sure that you believe that marriage is for life. We have so many years ahead of us; everything may change. This country may be in revolution soon and foreigners be forced to leave. You may find me an embarrassment. When we promise to stand by each other in good and bad times, you will mean it, won't you? You aren't just thinking of the next few years, are you?"

They had reached the car. The children were trailing them with a wary eye on Solomon. Solomon stopped and, facing Lorraine, took both her hands.

"I want you to be my wife for the rest of my life," he said simply. "I want us to face the difficulties ahead together. Is that clear enough for you?"

Lorraine felt a surge of happiness. She was convinced that God had brought Solomon to her: that their marriage was consecrated in heaven. If only meeting

The Love-Match

wasn't so difficult! In the country they were in, it was all but impossible for a man and a woman to get to know each other well before marriage. To be alone in a man's company was instantly suspect. Had Lorraine not been able to borrow the mission car sometimes on a Sunday afternoon they would hardly ever have been alone.

They got back into the car. The children drew nearer. One older boy called out something as Solomon got in and he turned angrily back in rebuke.

"What did he say?" Lorraine said, starting the engine.

"Oh...nothing!" Solomon answered. "Ignorant little beasts!"

But a little shadow had fallen across Lorraine's happiness.

That was so characteristic of her life these days: shadows and sunshine. There were days when she rejoiced to know Solomon was hers; when every verse in the Bible seemed to confirm her in her desire for marriage with him; when the touch of his hand would thrill her; when she lived for the smile in his eyes. At such times she felt like a girl again, though she was, in fact, in her mid-thirties. But there were times of shadows too.

She could hardly ever visit Solomon in his house where he lived with several other boys, but once his uncle and aunt were coming and so she was invited too. The visit had not been a success. The older people were made shy and embarrassed by her presence, and found her way of speaking their language difficult to understand. They had gone early, leaving Lorraine and Solomon together. That was the first time they had been able to embrace, to sit together in one chair, to kiss one another. Solomon had been very gentle as if afraid of

The Love-Match

frightening her, and she had been very careful not to let things go too far, but even then a shadow had fallen. There had been a snigger from the maid-servant in the next room and that had made Lorraine very aware that the walls were only wood and mud, with, no doubt, many convenient peepholes in them. She had got up, flushed and confused.

Other times when shadows fell were when the gap that lay between her education and Solomon's was referred to. Lorraine was a nurse and a trained midwife; Solomon, a twenty-year-old, unqualified teacher in a private school. In the evenings he was trying to finish his secondary schooling. Once he had asked her if she could find him a job in the Mission. Seeing her expression, he had quickly passed it off as a joke, but Lorraine had not yet told him that, to marry him, she must resign from the Mission. She reassured herself by telling herself that she could find a job somewhere in a government hospital until he finished his schooling. Then they would work together in evangelism or Bible teaching; or so she assured Stephen Karobo, pastor of the church they both attended.

She trusted Stephen, and although Dick and Frances Cameron of her Mission had made themselves very available to her for help and discussion, she preferred to talk to Stephen.

Stephen was a small, chunky African, with a brisk and cheerful manner. He had been educated in Sweden and had a Swedish wife.

"But there is a difference," he had said to Lorraine earlier. "Gertrud and I are nearly the same age; we know one another's countries well and, if anything, I am better educated than she. Those are all important things."

The Love-Match

"But the most important one is the will of God," Lorraine had said earnestly. "I feel it right to marry Solomon. We have prayed about it so much. Every verse of Scripture, every message we hear, seems to point to its rightness. Surely that is of first importance."

He regarded her seriously. "It is not for nothing," he said slowly, "that Satan is called the 'father of lies.' Let me say just one thing to you, Lorraine, and don't shut your ears to it. You are a missionary with many years of training behind you. Your work is valuable to this country. If you marry, I think you should marry one who, spiritually, will be your equal, if not your superior. No, don't speak," for he saw she was about to interrupt. "I know you say Solomon is all these things. All I say to you is: I don't know him and neither does the pastor of the church you say he belonged to in his own town. If he is the Christian you say he is, why is he not known in the Christian community? Why is he not already teaching the Bible? Be careful, and remember that it is more than possible for a man to counterfeit Christianity to gain his own ends."

"I know Solomon is the Lord's!" Lorraine was flushed and heated in his defense. "We have prayed and studied the Word together. He shares with me the desire to serve the Lord in witnessing and teaching."

"May it be so."

Someone knocked on the pastor's door and came in with a message. Lorraine took the opportunity to leave, blinking tears angrily away.

"You need a break," Dick Cameron said abruptly to her, when he met her later in the week. "I want you to go down to the South for a few weeks. Dorothy Faircloth needs dental treatment and you can take her

The Love-Match

place at the Jaranda clinic. It's not a busy time of year; should be quite a rest cure."

It was not uncommon for the mission medical personnel to have to cover for one another at times of sickness or vacation and Lorraine, reflecting that it would mean only a short separation from Solomon, agreed to go. Solomon saw her off on the bus, selecting the best seat for her and securing her luggage safely in the racks.

"I'll think of you every day," he promised her, taking her hand in farewell, "and when you return, I will have my parents here to meet you."

"Is that a promise?" she said, surprised.

"It is a promise."

Nancy Harrison, a teacher who lived with Dorothy, met Lorraine off the bus at Jaranda and whisked her off to the mission compound into a hot bath.

"I'm glad you could come," she said cheerfully. "That tooth really was giving Dorothy a lot of pain, but I just couldn't convince her that the clinic assistants could manage alone for a week or two. It was only when she heard you could come that she admitted that she'd be glad to go."

"Is the clinic very busy?" asked Lorraine, thankfully washing off the dust of the two-day journey.

"Not really...it's just that emergencies do happen, and they always happen just when no one's here." Nancy was cheerfully clattering dishes in the tiny kitchen. "And she was worried about Kathy Yosana."

"Kathy Yosana?" Lorraine stopped washing herself. "What about her?"

The Love-Match

"Do you know her? She used to be in the Baptist Mission and married a national over a year ago."

"I've...heard of her," Lorraine said. They were speaking through the thin wood of the bathroom door and Nancy did not hear the tension in her voice.

"Well, she's expecting a baby and she lives at Belbara, which is about sixteen kilometers from here. We're her nearest medical help. She sent a message in to Dorothy a week ago saying she thought she might need help at the birth."

"But why doesn't she go into the city…or at least come and stay here for a while?"

"Dorothy wanted her to do that, of course," Nancy answered. "She sent a note saying to come at once, but we got no answer. Dorothy sent another one two days ago, saying to send a message when labor started. That's why she didn't want to leave until you came."

"Is there a road to Belbara?" asked Lorraine.

"You can go about seven kilometers in the land rover. After that I'm afraid you have to walk. It's really rocky country around there. Her husband's something to do with road planning. That's why they're out there. Have you finished your bath? Supper's nearly ready."

"Won't be a moment." Lorraine stood up, wrapping a towel around herself. She had been startled to be reminded of Kathy. They had met just before Kathy's wedding to Petros Yosana, when Kathy had been glowing-eyed and deeply in love, and Lorraine had been impressed by her deep dedication to the Lord. Somehow it was another picture to think of her awaiting her first baby nine kilometers from the nearest road. Why had not Petros taken her into the city? Didn't he know first babies could be difficult, especially at Kathy's age?

The Love-Match

"How old is Kathy?" she asked Nancy when they were seated at the table.

"Nearly forty, I think." Nancy served out the tinned peas carefully. "Too old for a first baby anyway, according to Dorothy. Shall we say grace?"

Bowing her head for grace, Nancy did not see the faint flush that had risen to Lorraine's cheeks at her last words.

The call from Kathy came about ten in the morning, some three days later. It was brought to Lorraine in the clinic…a few scrawled words, obviously written by Kathy herself: "Please come soon. My pains are beginning."

"When did Mrs. Kathy start to be sick?" Lorraine asked of the boy who had ridden a horse in with the news.

"Early in the morning; dawn was just coming," was the answer.

Lorraine picked up the midwifery bag, took with her a clinic helper who said he knew the way, and started the journey. At the place where the trail left the road, a mule was waiting for her. She rode it through the rocky semi-desert to Belbara, a little town perched uncomfortably on the edge of the highlands. Tired and hot from riding through the midday sun, Lorraine arrived in the afternoon at the Yosanas' white-washed house. Kathy was up when she arrived, working in the kitchen. Bulky in pregnancy, with a white face lined with pain and hair dyed an unsuccessful dark-brown, she looked nearer fifty than forty. Tears welled in her eyes as she greeted Lorraine.

The Love-Match

"I have been praying that I wouldn't give birth until someone came to help me," she said. "The pains are coming about every twenty minutes now."

"Come and lie down," Lorraine told her. "Which is the coolest room in the house?"

"Our bedroom, probably. I've got a few things together." Kathy led the way and lay down thankfully on the bed, while Lorraine drew down the shades and brought some cold water to wash the sweat from Kathy's face.

"Where is Petros?" she asked.

"He'll be in soon, I expect. He's out surveying. They are planning a road from the road you came on right down into the lowlands," Kathy said between shut teeth.

"Don't try to talk more," Lorraine said gently. "Begin to relax a little. It'll soon be over."

Yosana, when he came in a little later, was a tall, fine-looking African, beautifully dressed in grey slacks and white shirt. He looked out of place so far from civilization.

"Age-wise," Lorraine thought, "they look more like mother and son than husband and wife." Unbidden, something Dick had said to her came back to her mind: "There is a greater difference between forty and fifty-five than between twenty-five and forty," he had said. So if they looked so different now, what would it be in fifteen years?

"I'm glad you can help Kathy," Yosana told her. "I try to tell her that women have babies all the time, but it doesn't seem to comfort her."

"Not at forty, they don't," thought Lorraine, but she said nothing.

The Love-Match

"Kathy thinks it's twins," said Yosana jovially, "but she hasn't been to hospital, so I don't know how she can be sure."

"Haven't you seen any doctor since you conceived?" said Lorraine worriedly to her.

"Petros thought it unnecessary," Kathy said. "I really have had no problems."

"I think I'll go out to dinner," Yosana told her. "I promised to meet the chief surveyor before he leaves tomorrow. See you later, Kathy."

"Very well," Kathy said without expression. She had seemed to hold back her pains while he was there, but once he left, she writhed on the hard bed. The evening was growing dark. A little servant girl brought them tea and offered food to Lorraine. Kathy would touch nothing. Lorraine lit some oil lamps. She was beginning to panic. What could she do if there were complications in the birth and no doctor at hand, no way of reaching help? A hundred terrible ideas presented themselves to her even as she leant over Kathy, soothing, trying to help her relax. Between the pains, Kathy whispered to her, "Don't be worried, Lorraine. God will do His will and if it is to take my life, there are many ways in which I will be grateful to Him."

Lorraine thought she must have misheard, and said, "Everything's going fine, Kathy. Don't worry. It'll be an hour or two yet."

Kathy gasped and twisted on the bed, seizing Lorraine's hands. As the spasm passed she sank down on the pillows again, her face wet with sweat.

"You don't think I mean it," she whispered feebly, "but I do. Don't ever be tempted, Lorraine, to do as I did....'

Lorraine felt herself suddenly in a nightmare. Her head swam.

The Love-Match

"What...what do you mean?" she said sharply.

"Don't marry a man of this people," said the hoarse whisper. "I thought he was a Christian, but we foreigners can be taken in so easily. No Christian girl would have married him...they know the good from the bad. We cannot tell...."

Lorraine tried to speak, but the words dried in her throat.

"I knew...I knew he wasn't a virgin when I married him," Kathy labored on. "None of them are, but I didn't know he would go on sleeping with them afterwards. I asked him once to stop...do you know what he said...?"

"No! No, hush! Don't tell me. You're delirious!" Lorraine caught her hands and spoke urgently.

"He said, 'What do you expect? You don't imagine I get any pleasure from playing around with a dried up old stick like you, do you?'"

"Hush!" Lorraine felt she could bear no more. Kathy was caught up in a fresh paroxysm and writhed, moaning. Lorraine hurried into the kitchen where she found the servant girl waiting silently.

"Have you the boiling water I asked for?" she said, and the girl showed her the pan with her instruments boiling in it. Lorraine took them out and laid them down to dry in the sterilizer. She would have liked to stay there in the kitchen, but she heard Kathy cry and reluctantly returned.

Back in the bedroom she started talking lightly about news in the city, anything, just to talk, to stop Kathy talking and humiliating herself further, but Kathy was not listening. She had kept back her thoughts for so long that it seemed she could not stop herself now, and she talked on, never knowing that each word hurt Lorraine more than she could say.

The Love-Match

"I knew others had found it didn't work," she said weakly, "but I believed we were different. I was so certain it was the Lord's will; I saw it as a key to the hearts of the people whom I loved. We would serve the Lord together."

Despite herself, Lorraine bent forward and asked a question, "Well, wasn't it a key to the hearts of the people? Do they not accept you as one of themselves when you live among them as an equal?"

Kathy smiled, but with bitterness.

"They will never accept me except as a foreigner—a joke, a person to look at. My husband is well known in the bars of the town. How can they respect me, who can't keep my husband...ohhh!"

Her words ended in a gasp. Lorraine saw she might begin to need help, and called to the servant, "Are there women who could come in?"

They came, two or three neighbors, and helped hold Kathy steady. They looked compassionate but resigned. Death in childbirth was common in their lives. Kathy began to scream and Lorraine shut her ears to it.

Yosana came in, drunk, at 2:30 in the morning. Lorraine met him at the door. Kathy, drained and spent, was sleeping heavily.

"You have two daughters," Lorraine told him bluntly.

"Two useless girls?" he muttered, trying to focus his eyes. "What...what damn good are they?"

The Love-Match

Five weeks later, back in the city, she told the story to Stephen Karobo.

"The Lord was good to enable you to reach her in time," he said. "I'm sorry she suffered so much."

"But I had to leave her there," Lorraine said. "What will happen to her?"

"Dorothy will call and see her on her return."

"But what of the future? She can't go on living like that."

"For a time the children will compensate for much. Then they will all go to Canada. It is probably what Yosana wants."

"You mean he married her to get abroad!" Lorraine said bitterly. "I know that is what they all say. But Solomon does not want to go abroad. He wants to serve the Lord here!"

Stephen said nothing. Lorraine got up restlessly and went to the window, playing with the cords of the venetian blinds.

"It wouldn't be like that! It couldn't be!" she said. But phrases Kathy used kept coming back to her…"I was sure it was right"…"I believed we were different"… "We would serve the Lord together." She went back to the desk where Stephen sat watching her with understanding and patience.

"There are girls living in Solomon's house," she said abruptly. "I know, because I heard one of them giggling. He has no sisters. Who are they?"

"Servant girls, I expect," he answered. "Unmarried men always have girls to cook for them and do the housework."

"And to sleep with them?" she said with difficulty.

"And to sleep with them."

The Love-Match

Lorraine sat and buried her head in her arms.

"It is not true! Not true!" she said in a muffled voice. "Solomon is not like that!"

There was silence again. Then she looked up.

"What shall I do?" she said.

"I remember a poem in your language," Stephen said reflectively.

> *"To every man there openeth*
> *A high way and a low;*
> *And every man decideth*
> *The way his soul shall go."*

"I think you are at a crossroad, Lorraine. No one ever pretended the high way was an easy way."

"But if...I give him up...cancel the marriage plans...how shall I face life again?"

"As everyone has to who has ever lived. No one's life is quite what they want it to be," Stephen answered her. "We must build it cheerfully around what God has given, not spend time yearning for what is not."

"But I thought God had given this. I still think it is the will of God to marry."

"It is never easy to find the will of God," said the pastor kindly. "We have areas in our lives where Satan can pretend to be an angel of light, areas where we are very likely to make mistakes. A woman in your position, Lorraine, might find it very difficult to make a right decision about marriage. That is why God has given us friends and counselors. I think you should listen to them. If those who know both you and Solomon counsel against this marriage, I would be very, very careful before I went ahead."

The Love-Match

Lorraine's eyes filled with tears. She sat staring at the desktop.

"Jesus was unmarried," Stephen suddenly said gently. "Had you thought of that? We are taught that He was a whole man, tempted like we are. Do you think He had no sexual desires? He left them unfulfilled so He could do the work He was sent to do. Perhaps that is what God is asking of you. Perhaps that is His highest way for you."

"But love cannot be turned on and off like a tap." Lorraine's voice was unsteady. "Even if I never see him again, I will still love him."

"Ah yes, love." Stephen leant back in his chair. "I had forgotten for the moment that you have been brought up to choose your mates on that unstable and wavering emotion. This is one of the times I think it better to do as we do: to let love grow after marriage. No, I cannot help you here. It will be a wound and then a scar that you may carry through life."

Life! Life without Solomon: to be as she was before, with no end in view....

*"To every man there openeth
A high way and a low;
And every man decideth
The way his soul shall go."*

Lorraine sat quite still. She really had little doubt now which was the high and which the low. The only thing she didn't know was whether she had courage to choose the right one.

Chapter 5
The Last Night

To my honored father, Elhana Goru.

I am going to write to you tonight, Father, as if you understood what I was saying: as if you were the father I want and need, instead of an old man in a torn, earth-colored shirt, plodding behind the oxen on that stony hillside. You'll never see the letter, Father, for I write with the door locked and a charcoal fire nearby. It is dangerous, these days, to record the true thoughts of the heart.

I know you try to understand me, Father. You came into town last week to try again, didn't you?—to try and communicate with this strange son of yours.

I saw you suddenly, standing there by the rails of the bank as I came out for lunch, in your best shirt and trousers, and even in shoes, which you must have borrowed for the occasion: humbly standing there, making no sign of recognition, in case I didn't want to know you.

Mind you, Father, if I'd been with Kalehe, or another friend, I don't know what I would have done, but as it

The Last Night

was, I was alone, and I know you were touched when I knelt to kiss your feet. You see, I am sorry, Father, sorry that I am offending you and hurting you, but I am still going to marry Persai.

They made you come, of course, my mother and my aunt, for they have had my future wife selected since my infancy. You might have been content to let me choose for myself, but she's a forceful woman, my mother. You raised me and I saw tears in your eyes. I know you want to understand, Father. I wish, oh I wish, that I could really make you see what is troubling me and my generation in this big city, what is making me so different from what you and your brothers were as children.

Do you know where your only son spent last night, Father? In prison! Herded in with thieves, liars, beggars and vagabonds, because I was unwise enough to tell the truth! Let me tell you what happened. There was this little trade-van driven by a young man in blue overalls, and it was parked at the side of the road while the young man was unloading something from it. Suddenly a big, shiny Mercedes car, parked ahead of him, backed right into the van and smashed its headlights and the front of the bonnet. You know how quickly people gather when something like that happens. I was held in the crowd. A tall man got out of the Mercedes and shouted that the other fellow had driven into him and should be arrested and fined. When the van-driver had not even been in the driver's seat! The young man was so helpless, Father: terrified at the damage done to the van, confused at the shouting and quite innocent. I stepped forward.

"It is lies!" I shouted. "This man backed his car right into the van!"

The Last Night

The tall man looked at me and I recognized him. I suppose I dare not write his name here, but he is one of the most powerful of the ruling class. He said, "You would do well to forget that remark, young man."

The van-driver clutched at my arm, "Brother, help me! You saw it all. This is my employer's van. I will lose my job...lose my means of living, if he is believed. My children will starve! For my wife and children's sake, testify for me!"

I suppose I was a fool, but I saw the nobleman smile at the driver's agitation. I saw him openly hand out dollar notes to the watching crowd and then turn back to me.

"I do not lack witnesses that this fellow drove into me," he said calmly.

The crowd began to shout.

"No! No! We saw it all. The fellow drove right into the car."

The police had arrived by this time and I saw a big policeman grab the van-driver and twist his arms behind his back so that he cried out. I lost my head. "You evil man!" I shouted. "You, who are meant to lead others, lie and bribe your way out of a situation and don't care who you hurt in doing it. This man's livelihood is at stake and you want him to suffer for a mistake you made!"

Well, Father, I suppose you will be horrified that I could speak like that to one of the great of the land. I know you will understand that it was useless. I saw the police begin to close in on me and, foolishly, I turned to run. They followed me, of course, everyone did. One of the police even fired a pistol. They caught me easily and

The Last Night

beat me across the back and the calves of my legs for running away. They took me to the police station.

"Learn to obey the police!" one shouted, and slapped me in the face.

In the cells it would have gone hard with me had I not had enough money with me to escape beatings from the other prisoners. As it was, they let me lie on the dirty stone floor, untouched except by their spittle and foul language.

Next day I paid a bribe of fifty dollars to the police captain for my release. I hung my head and said nothing when he said he'd heard that I had a complaint to make against an arrest. I hated myself for it, Father, but I had done enough. I could not face a long court case that would inevitably be lost before it began. I walked out, paying a further five dollars to the gate-keeper, and left the van-driver to his fate. I suppose he will become one of the crowd of beggars in the city streets when they let him out of prison.

What can I do, Father, when I live in such a city: where truth is replaced by bribes and the very leaders are corrupt? I know you would say I should return to you and work the land; try to forget the oppression, the wickedness of the city. I wish I could but it is impossible. I love my country; I care who governs it and how. If those of us who value truth and freedom leave the cities, it will mean we have condoned the wrong and shut our eyes to oppression and injustice. I cannot do it.

Freedom! You probably know more of freedom than I do, Father...out there, trying to live off the soil with a heavy stick and two oxen. We shout about it for other countries, but dare not suggest we do not have it ourselves. Everything we do, everything we say here, is

The Last Night

noted and recorded by the authorities. Even this morning I was searched on my way to work and my ID card was demanded. They only let me go because I was a worker and not a student. The students here are the most abused of all. Let them question what is happening and they disappear and cannot be traced. No wonder they are afraid.

Yes, afraid! Do you wonder, Father, that even your tall, strong, and wholly beautiful son is afraid? Do you know how infectious fear can be...the turned head, the sudden silences, the quick heartbeat? If you are thought to harbor resentment against the regime, you can be in prison the next day. There are black mail-boxes now at the main crossroads of the city. Anyone may denounce someone else and put the letter in one of those boxes... and then there are the whips, the torture. Can you wonder, Father, that you are the only one to whom I dare write these thoughts?

I write tonight, Father, because tomorrow I may not be here. I am leaving; for America. Something else has happened which one day I will tell you about; I have become a Christian, and God is real to me at last. He is so different from the God I have been brought up to believe in...He is nothing to do really with that old, decaying building we used to go to and the old, drunken priest (forgive me) who took our money and told us our sins were forgiven. He is a Spirit, a Lover, a Redeemer. It is partly this that has made me decide to marry Persai. I want to marry someone who worships God as I worship Him. I hope she will be able to follow me to America in a month or two. Do not be afraid of her; when you know her, you will love her and she will be a good and faithful daughter-in-law to you.

The Last Night

I know you will not want me to go abroad, Father, but I must. I don't know enough yet to fight these rulers, this way of life. Once, when we still had friends in the police, I heard a police officer say of the students, "They only know what they don't want. They should save their rioting until they know what they do!" It's a fair taunt and I am ready to be silent for the time being…until I know something of the ways of government. I remember reading once of a speech of an American leader where he talked of a "government of the people, by the people, for the people." Perhaps, in America, I will see what that means. It is called the "free West"; perhaps I can see what their freedom is.

It is difficult to get permission to leave this country, but I must go now, before it is impossible and the borders are finally closed. Missionaries are helping me. You don't know any foreigners, do you, Father? You would find them strange if you did. They agree to send us abroad reluctantly, for in their lands education is free for all and they know nothing of the frustrations of not getting a place in school, or of schools being closed for half the year because the government is afraid of student riots. But at last they have agreed to help me, and at last my papers are through.

I wish, just once before I leave, that I could come to you, Father, and sit at your feet. I want to recall the old traditions of our land before I leave it: the songs of the people, the unchanging heritage of the countryside. Here in the city the world is changing…factories, apartment-complexes, multi-story car-parks, televisions, washing-machines, tape-recorders…. They call us a "developing country," but leave it to us to ask, "developing into what?" We cannot stop it, Father, for the world is moving on and we must move with it, but I am afraid

The Last Night

that we might be losing something fine and precious that we'll never find again....

I know I won't find all the answers abroad, Father. If there is good there, it will yet have to be fitted into our land when I return. Don't be afraid that I won't return. This is my land; it sings in my heart, beats in my blood. That's why I knelt to you there in the street, Father. I knelt in homage to what you have given me: my heritage of Africa. Africa will yet be great among the nations of the world: great for its true freedoms of mind and heart.

This letter, crumpled and unsigned, was found on the floor of an empty house, where a splintered door swung loosely on its hinges.

Chapter 6
An Axe at the Roots

The bell rang at the door and Rhonda laid down her pen and went to answer it. Opening the fly screens she smiled at Sirane, the tall and handsome young School Administrator.

"Hello, Sirane. Come in."

Sirane did so with his easy grace and pleasant smile. He was carrying a pile of school registers.

"Could some of us come and see you after lunch today, Miss Bailey? There are one or two things we want to discuss with you."

"Yes, of course." It was a common enough request and Rhonda thought nothing of it. "Where do you want to meet? Here?"

"If that's convenient."

"Yes; I'll expect you about half past one. How many of you?"

Sirane seemed unsure of himself for the first time.

"Just some of the office staff and...a few of the teachers," he said.

Something seemed wrong in the way he answered and Rhonda asked, "What was it about?"

An Axe at the Roots

"Oh...just something we wanted you to see. May we tell you then?"

It wasn't quite a straight answer but Rhonda had known Sirane since he had been a serious-faced little boy in one of the mission schools in the countryside. It was she who had encouraged him to get secondary education and employed him afterwards as a junior teacher. Later he had shown such aptitude in business that he had become chief administrator of the girls' boarding school of which she was principal. She trusted him now and said lightly, "All right. I'll expect you."

At half past one Rhonda was surprised to see nearly all the African teachers and three or four office staff outside her house. She opened the screens again and beckoned to them to come up the steps. They filed into her sitting-room and found themselves seats. For the first time she wondered if there was serious trouble on the horizon. She looked at Sirane, but he had managed to sit in a corner, unobtrusively. Obviously he wasn't going to speak first.

"Well?" she said. "Which of you is going to tell me why you've come?"

As she looked around she suddenly realized that none of them was meeting her eyes. They were nearly all young men; most of them, like Sirane, were those she had taught herself and seen grow into manhood in her twenty-four years of missionary service. One girl was there, the wife of a Science teacher, but the other two female staff had not come. She saw Sirane frown pointedly at the Math teacher, Namonga, and looked at Namonga expectantly. Unaccountably her heart began to race.

An Axe at the Roots

Namonga cleared his throat and took from a file he was carrying a printed sheet of paper.

"We wanted to show this to you, Miss Bailey," he said slowly. "We felt you should see it."

She held out her hand. The paper was typed. It began, *"The paper on which is written the accusations against Miss R. Bailey, Principal of Hope Mission School."*

A numbness crept over Rhonda; her throat went dry and she had to force herself to keep her hand steady and her eyes focused on the paper as she read, *"The staff who write their names on this paper believe Miss Bailey should apologize for these things and resign from being principal of this school.*

Accusations
1. Misusing for her own advantage the money paid as fees.
2. Insulting African traditions.
3. Degrading members of staff.
4. Unkindness to students.
5. Unfairness in grading.
6. Prejudice against office staff...."

The paper suddenly blurred and Rhonda knew she could read no more then. She tried to keep her voice steady, telling herself fiercely inside, "Don't let them see you weep," and said, "I will read this paper over carefully, but just tell me one thing. When have I ever insulted or degraded you?"

She looked across at Sirane, but he still refused to look at her. There was an uncomfortable silence. At length Sirane muttered, "Vania, you speak."

Vania! Rhonda looked at him. He had been a crippled orphan boy in the mission orphanage in whom she

An Axe at the Roots

had taken a special interest. An American doctor had operated so that he could walk, stiffly, but erect. She had paid for his expenses in a Teacher Training College and finally employed him as an English teacher. Now he looked sullen and angry. He said roughly, "You call us mice!"

"Call you...." Rhonda began in utter amazement, when he added, "And said you were the cat. We were playing when you weren't there."

Rhonda's mind went back to a staff meeting in the spring term. She had been called to the phone in the middle and when she had returned had found the young teachers laughing and practicing a kind of indoor golf. She had laughed with them, but had she used lightly that old English proverb? She must have done so, before she had called the meeting back to order.

"Vania, that was just a joke," she said gently. "It is an English saying. You misunderstood it."

"There are other things," said Namonga after a moment. Rhonda felt strongly that, although he was trying not to say anything, Sirane was the true director of the meeting. She had not caught his signal to Namonga, but she saw that most of the staff seemed embarrassed and uncomfortable, unwilling to speak unless prompted by him. She turned the paper over. All their signatures were on it: even, down at the bottom, unobtrusively, Sirane's. She looked across at him and said steadily, "Why don't you tell me these other things, Sirane? You brought this meeting together, didn't you?"

He glanced at her flushed face and looked away.

"We have arranged who will speak" was all he said.

One by one about six or seven of the teachers spoke of incidents in school that had taken place in the last year or two. One—"insulting our national flag"—even

An Axe at the Roots

went back over two years, to a time when one of the girls had fainted during the flag-raising ceremony and Rhonda had helped her away. Most were based on truth, as that had been; but others, such as the misuse of money and the accusation of saying things against the country's government, were not.

Hearing them speak as if through a thick curtain, Rhonda kept her eyes on the paper in her hand. It was ridiculous, unreal, monstrous, that these boys whom she had known from childhood, to whom she had given the best and strongest years of her life, should have suddenly become strangers, wanting to humiliate and destroy her. Their voices saying these things were half-ashamed, but there was underneath an unmistakable note of bitterness, even hatred against her.

She listened to it all with an unchanging face. Now that the first shock was over, self-possession came back. When no-one had spoken for a few minutes she said, "Has anyone else anything to say?"

There was silence.

"Then I will see you all later. I will think this over. In the meantime, classes will continue as usual."

They rose, but as they went out she spoke to Sirane.

"Sirane, will you remain behind?"

He hesitated, looking down at her undecidedly, but then said, "I have nothing to add to what has been said," and went to the door. There, he turned back. "It has not perhaps been made plain to you," he said quietly, "that copies of these accusations have been sent to the mission headquarters, the Bishop of this province, and the Ministry of Education," and he went out.

Rhonda sat down at the polished dining-room table, her square, homely face set rigid. The sun streamed in,

An Axe at the Roots

at its hottest just then. A few flies buzzed angrily at the windows.

The room was full of memories of the twenty-four years she had spent in the country: wood-carvings, a monkey-skin rug, school photographs, and a picture one of the art teachers had presented to her last New Year. It was a beautiful room, a restful room, where many young Christians had found friendship and counsel, but Rhonda saw none of it.

She thought, not for the first time, that heartache was a real ache: a kind of tightness in her breast. She could not move. All these years she had loved them, helped them, taught them, made them what they were, and now they could do this to her. Sirane. She remembered the difficulty he had had over marrying the girl of his choice, the hours he had spent pouring his heart out to her about it. In the end they had had the wedding in the school with her acting as the mother of the bride, because the bride's own parents had refused to let her marry a Christian. She was god-mother to their first little one. She remembered how she had fought to get him the use of a mission car and a car allowance, the furniture she had given them when they first set up house; and now he had done this. He had looked at her as if she were a stranger, a foreigner; he had incited the others to accuse her and drive her away.

She could not cry. All she could do, out of dry and burning lips, was to whisper, "Oh, Christ. You must understand what this means to me. Help me somehow to live through it."

The bell rang for afternoon school. She stood, a short, stocky figure with graying hair, and picking up her books went down the steps and across to the school.

An Axe at the Roots

She moved as if she was in a daze: her eyes full of a suffering unlike anything she had ever known.

...REGRET TO ANNOUNCE THAT FLIGHT NUMBER EA 432 TO LONDON WILL DEPART APPROXIMATELY TWO HOURS LATE. PASSENGERS IN TRANSIT MAY LEAVE THE TRANSIT LOUNGE AND HAVE DINNER IN THE MAIN RESTAURANT.

Rhonda heard the announcement but it did not really register. She was at Athens airport, on her way home to London, sitting in the transit lounge with the stiff, expressionless face she had learnt to wear in the last months, to cover the pain.

It was three and a half months after the trouble in the school. She was going on what the Mission called "early furlough." She privately doubted if she would ever return. She could not think of any part of the three and a half months without pain. The mission elders had come to the school; they had been joined by the local church elders and pastors in an attempt to solve the problems. It was the custom of the country that others from outside were called in when there were difficulties between two parties. But the teachers refused to withdraw their accusations; it was only thanks to the director of the Mission, who was on good terms with the Minister of Education, that the accusations had not reached high government officials. Only one accusation they had been forced to withdraw: the charge of misusing money. The school treasurer kept good records and was able to account for everything that had passed through Rhonda's hands.

An Axe at the Roots

Rhonda had had to sit, day after day, listening to every innocent remark she had made being wrongly construed; she was accused of saying things that she knew she could never have said. Embarrassed schoolgirls were examined and their evidence sifted. Constantly with her was the wretchedness of the realization that those whom she had loved most had turned against her, with, to her, unbelievable and incomprehensible hatred.

She had gone on holiday to the Mission rest-home and experienced the pity and sympathy of other missionaries. That was almost worse than being at the school, for she could not explain. She did not know what had gone wrong.

"Miss Bailey, are you not going to have dinner?"

Rhonda looked up, startled to see a tall, graying African looking down at her, his hat in his hand.

"Archdeacon Rassa!" she said in surprise. "Are you on this flight? I didn't see you at the airport."

"I was there," the man answered, smiling, his overcoat falling open to show his clerical collar. "I sat at the back of the plane. Will you come and have dinner with me?"

He picked up her bag and shepherded her across the lounge towards the restaurant.

"I wondered if you would recognize me," he said as they sat down. "I was watching you across the room and thinking it must be over eight years since we met."

"I wouldn't forget you," Rhonda answered. "We were so proud to hear you had been given the archdeaconry; and glad too, though it was the Mission's loss."

"Ah yes, I owe a great deal to the Mission," the Archdeacon said gently. "I remember being the very worst little boy in your class!"

An Axe at the Roots

"Don't!" Rhonda said suddenly and tears sprang to her eyes. "Don't be grateful, Archdeacon. I couldn't bear it."

He was silent. The first course was brought in and they began to eat. After a moment Rhonda said abruptly, "You know, Rassa, don't you? Why I'm going home, I mean, and what happened at the school?"

"Yes," he answered simply. "That's why I came to talk to you. God meant us to be together on this plane. You should not leave, Miss Bailey, bearing in your heart such grief and bitterness."

"I have tried not to," she said in a low voice. "I have tried to tell myself that the Lord suffered misunderstanding and wrongful accusation, that He was turned out by His own people and tribe; but still I am bitter."

"Because you have been hurt."

"Hurt, yes, and I am so confused. I'd tried to give them everything I could, everything they needed to be independent citizens of their country. I loved them and I thought they loved me. They were as my family to me; I thought of them as my sons and daughters in the Lord...but all the time they must have been hating me. I know I made mistakes, but why did they never tell me them? Why couldn't they have come as Christians and discussed them quietly with me instead of publicly humiliating me and rejoicing because I suffered?" She paused, aware of her rising voice, and went on more quietly, "All through the last months I have asked myself what I have done wrong, what I would do differently if I had all my missionary life over again. I don't know the answer; I honestly tried to give them all I could."

The Archdeacon, watching her, laid down his fork.

"You have not been 'hated,' as you put it, all these years, Miss Bailey. You know that. It is the last years that

An Axe at the Roots

have brought changes to our country. Free Africa sees what it can do by acting together as a group. Few can resist power, especially the power to injure and humiliate a white."

"I never think of my color," Rhonda said dully.

"That is because you are white," Archdeacon Rassa said simply. "I want to talk frankly with you, Miss Bailey. You will permit me?"

"Of course."

"You have just said, 'I tried to give them all I could,' and that is true. Those young teachers, many of them, owe their schooling, their clothing, their jobs, their homes, some of them their health, to you. Can you imagine what it is like to carry that burden of gratitude to a foreigner in your own country? Would you like, in England, to owe that to an African immigrant, to have to smile and say thank you, to have to do as they say and not contradict them in case they withdraw some of their support? Would you like to have to go humbly to beg for an extra favor: perhaps the fare somewhere to see a relative?"

Rhonda stared at him. He went on, still speaking gently and quietly, his voice quite free of bitterness.

"You will say you didn't want conformity, gratitude, but to whom do you give more? To the boy who takes, and turns his back, or to the boy who smiles and says 'thank you,' who is helpful and polite. And always at the back of their minds is the thought, 'Why should I be grateful? It is the accident of birth that has put her in that position, not any superiority of mind or body.'"

"Do *you* feel like that towards us?" Rhonda asked.

"No, but I used to. The Lord has shown me that bitterness allowed to remain and fester in my heart will hurt me more than those I feel bitter about," the

An Axe at the Roots

Archdeacon answered calmly. "But such feelings are still near the surface. You say you don't think about color, but I say to you: think and pray, for there is, in any white, the feeling of supremacy, and, in any black, the feeling of injustice, that needs all the grace the Lord can give to erase."

"But you believe and I believe that we stand before the Lord as equally sinners in His sight. I have lived, or I have tried to live, by that principle," protested Rhonda.

"We are building," said the gentle African, "on a foundation that has already been laid, not by us, of generations of white supremacy. You dislike our capital city, I know. Beggars stop you to beg for money, street-boys beg to watch your car and then steal from it, women stop you to ask if they may be your servant; your supremacy is established from the moment you land."

"But...." began Rhonda, then stopped helplessly.

"I am on the way to your country now," went on the Archdeacon. "Will white people beg money from me? Will the children of my neighbors beg to watch my car? Will I have white servants? Are there schools with a black principal and white staff, or business offices with black directors and white office-staff?" He stopped. The Greek waiter served them with the next course. When he had gone, the African looked at Rhonda and smiled.

"I am telling you these things," he said, "to help you understand that the difference between a missionary and a national is one put there, not by individuals, but by a whole cultural history. It is not something that can disappear quickly; perhaps it never will; but maybe to understand a little is to forgive."

"So what shall we do?" asked Rhonda. "Stop trying? Close our mission work and leave it all to you?"

An Axe at the Roots

"Where you can, yes. Missions must cease to lead and direct nationals and national churches the moment they have the ability to lead themselves."

"But we are doing that! All our work is being nationalized. I was the only white person in the entire school and when I retired the school would have been entirely African-run."

"When—you—retired?" the Archdeacon said slowly. "When would that have been…seven, eight, nine years ahead? Is the ability of the African director somehow dependent on your retirement?"

Rhonda flushed and was silent. He looked kindly upon her and waited for her answer. Rhonda thought hard. Had she been unwilling to let go? Had she consciously or unconsciously had an eye to her pension rights if she kept going for a few more years until she was sixty? Had she, who had trusted God for her whole life work, been unable to trust Him to find her employment during her later years?

"For those missionaries whose calling is the nurture and upbuilding of the church overseas," said Rassa, "there is only one way open to them: train the national and go. Do not stay beside them because you like the authority, the climate of the country, the security of a job; do not run things for them. Give them what you can in skills and in knowledge, and then leave it to them. Don't let them be greatly in debt to you. Let them know you are being paid to teach them, that you enjoy their country, that you are taking as well as giving. Above all, be ready to go."

"You think we cannot work side by side?"

"For the moment there can be no 'side by side,'" he answered. "Perhaps in thirty, forty years; who knows?

An Axe at the Roots

A few generations cannot change a cultural concept still being taught to your young in England."

"But we are Christians," Rhonda said. "Does that make no difference?"

"Only in that you have learnt to cover your deep feelings with the right words, even sometimes the right actions. True equality of black and white will only come when these are replaced by the right thoughts. Then you will no longer need to guard your words and actions; they will come easily to you."

Rhonda thought that over. She was an innately honest person and things were slipping into focus as the Archdeacon spoke.

"You are going to England to speak at Keswick?" she asked suddenly.

"Yes."

"Doesn't that show our willingness to honor you, to learn from you?"

"Yes; it shows a...certain kind of honor," Rassa replied slowly and smiled at her look of puzzlement. "I expect we will meet in the mission house party," he said. "Watch carefully and ask yourself how you were treated in the African church when you first arrived."

The Keswick Convention took place the next month. Rhonda had thought a good deal of the conversation she had had with Archdeacon Rassa at Athens airport, but had not seen him again in England. As he had predicted, they met at the mission house party.

There was a welcome meeting the first evening. The Archdeacon was given a place of honor and the big, jovial Home Secretary of the Mission made a great deal

An Axe at the Roots

of "our brother from across the seas." Rhonda glanced around the room. There were others there, from Scandinavia, from Australia. Why weren't they being welcomed too? The Archdeacon was asked to say a few words. He got to his feet:

"It is my pleasure," he said, "to be with you, for had it not been for you and those like you I may never have come to know the Lord Jesus Christ as my Savior."

His eye caught Rhonda's and he smiled at her, seeming to say, "If you want this and need it, it costs me nothing to give it to you."

Later, in the more informal part of the evening, some ladies surrounded Archdeacon Rassa. "Sing something, Mr. Rassa. Sing something in your language for us!"

"As if he were a performing dog," thought Rhonda, drawing near the group. "Can I imagine a visiting clergyman from England being asked to do that in an African gathering?" To her over-sensitive eyes there seemed something very wrong in the scene: a patronizing, over-effort of fellowship that could and should have been offered as naturally and simply as the members of the house party accepted church leaders of their own people.

The Archdeacon, loving and understanding as ever, obliged, and sang a revival chorus in a rather out-of-tune tenor. He apologized for his voice and the ladies laughed sympathetically.

"Oh, isn't he sweet?" Rhonda distinctly heard one of them say to her neighbor.

Hot and embarrassed, she left the room. Just outside the door she met another missionary, Francis Hart, a man in his early thirties who had been working in a neighboring country to hers in Africa.

An Axe at the Roots

"Is Archdeacon Rassa in there, Rhonda?" he asked.

"Yes," she said bitterly. "Singing a song to the ladies of the mission supporters!"

He raised an eyebrow and pushed open the door. They looked together. The Archdeacon was writing out some words in his language for the group of admiring people.

"It's all wrong!" Rhonda said fiercely. "We're treating him as a tamed savage, not as a brother in the Lord!"

Francis looked at her with comprehension.

"He'll understand," he said. "There's not much Archdeacon Rassa can't take."

"But why can't we be natural? Why do we have this patronizing friendship? It's almost worse than ignoring him."

Francis shrugged. "He's black. Probably the only one the good ladies have ever talked to."

"Oh, is there no end to this barrier of black and white?" Rhonda said hopelessly.

Francis caught the edge of desperation in her tone, and did not treat her question as merely rhetorical. He closed the door again and they stood facing each other in the hall.

"My father used to read Kipling to me when I was a boy," he said. "I learnt a lot of it by heart. Some lines that came back to me when I first went out to Africa are:

'Oh, East is East, and West is West,
 and never the twain shall meet,
Till Earth and Sky stand presently
 at God's great Judgment Seat;

An Axe at the Roots

But there is neither East nor West,
> Border, nor Breed, nor Birth,

When two strong men stand face to face,
> though they come from the ends of the earth!'"

He smiled at Rhonda's look of puzzlement.

"I interpret that spiritually," he said. "Men and women strong in Christ. I decided, when I arrived in Africa, that I was too much a child of my culture to be able to do anything about the color bar in my own strength. Only Christ could take away that innate superiority that the Africans knew was there. Only He could make me stop paying lip-service to the idea that we are equal in mind, body and spirit, and help me to *believe* it is true." He paused and looked down at Rhonda. "When we are strong in the Lord and in the power of His might," he said more slowly, searching for words, "and when we meet a brother or sister who also has grown in the Lord, then only do I know what it is to feel no sense of color."

The door opened and Archdeacon Rassa stood in the opening.

"Francis!" he said, and his face lit up.

Francis turned from Rhonda to embrace his friend and they went off together.

Rhonda went slowly into the now deserted sitting-room. She did not know Francis very well, but was deeply grateful to him for his brief words. "If strength in Christ is the answer," she thought, "then it is not beyond my reach. He is willing to do His part, I know."

An Axe at the Roots

She bent and picked up a pamphlet advertising work overseas. It was not too late to begin again, in the new world of mission. After all, God was a God of new beginnings.

Chapter 7
Between the Lines

The Thanksgiving dinner was over. The children had run off to play with some other missionary children outside. The four adults sat, uncomfortably replete, around the table that Pat Fraser had brought from Illinois when she and Howard had first gone to the mission field fourteen years before.

"Well, that's the strangest Thanksgiving dinner I can remember!" commented Dorothy with a laugh. "With the temperature in the eighties and all the flowers in bloom outside."

"I guess it isn't quite like what we'd do at home..." began Pat apologetically.

"Oh, Honey, Dorothy didn't mean that in criticism," Art said quickly, patting her hand kindly. "That was a great meal. How you managed to get a turkey out here, I just don't know."

Pat didn't know either. Putting that Thanksgiving dinner together to entertain their home church pastor and his wife had cost her what it usually took to feed her family of four for over a week. They'd have to practice some economy when they'd gone all right!

Between the Lines

"We can't live just like Americans here," Howard said, "but we try to keep up a few of the home traditions for the sake of the children. We don't want them to grow up without any knowledge of their country."

"No, no. Of course not!" agreed Art. "And we're glad to see it. This will really be something to tell the church back home. Thanksgiving dinner in the tropics. Well, Dorothy, I expect you'd like to put your feet up for a while. Howard and I must have a little talk together."

Dorothy looked a little taken aback at this sudden dismissal, but took it graciously and said she must certainly lie down for a little while. She and Pat went off, leaving the men together.

"Well now, Howard, come and sit down," said Art genially, getting up from the table. "We've had a great month out here, seeing the work and the national church, and all that our money is doing to forward God's work. You all couldn't have been kinder, and I want you to know we really appreciate everything you and Pat have done in entertaining us."

"We were honored to have you, Pastor," Howard said, following his guest into the sitting area of the room and managing to trip over a small footstool before subsiding gratefully into a chair. "I'm glad you could come out and see some of the work. I'm afraid the situation at Bamor was a little disappointing for you...."

"Oh...we expect to see a few difficulties as well as matters for praise," Art said, dismissing with a wave of the hand a situation that had cost the mission and the missionaries in Bamor months of heartache and days of conferences. "We'll be able to share the good things with the folks at home. That'll be a great help to their giving. Which reminds me to ask you, Howard, how are you managing with money? Does giving keep up? You must be doing all right if you can put on a spread like we've just had."

Howard looked at him in some dismay. He had tried to suggest to Pat that it might not be wise to make such a feast for Art and Dorothy, but Pat was an American housewife and wouldn't hear of their entertaining guests for Thanksgiving dinner by killing a couple of hens, as they usually did for any festival.

"Well, as a matter of fact, we are in some difficulty," he said awkwardly. "Rosemary's school fees...."

"Of course, the children are growing up, aren't they?" Art said heartily. "People at home don't always realize that children's expenses increase as they get older."

"Pastor," Howard said desperately, his round face getting even redder. "This is hard to share, but we are already in debt to the school here for about a thousand dollars. Even with Pat teaching full-time at the American Community School, we can hardly manage. We're getting less from the church now than when we came, fourteen years ago, and there is just no comparison between what it cost to live then and what it costs now. Could you explain this to the church at home? I really don't think we can stay here without more help."

Art looked a trifle embarrassed.

"Well, we'll certainly tell this to the church at home," he said. "Of course, sending Dorothy and me on this visit to see you all has been a big drain on the missionary budget. But I'll certainly mention it. Yes, we'll tell them what you said. As a matter of fact, Howard, that leads me to something I've been meaning to say to you. I know you'll understand that I'm only passing on things from the people in the church. There've been—that is—some people, some of the elders, just occasionally ask me about what you're doing out here. Now I know your work in the tape-recording ministry and...er...photography and things is very important, and people sure appreciate you. I hear the African brethren say on every side how good you are to them. But, you see, people like to kind of know that their money goes to the salvation of sinners...."

"I know what you're saying, Pastor," Howard said quietly. "I hoped during your time here you would be interested to come into the office and see just what it is I'm doing."

"Yes, yes, I wish there had been time," Art was looking uncomfortable, "but, after all, you have explained to me the set-up in this...er...mass-media center and we sure appreciate the movies you send back to us from time to time. Of course, I don't fully understand all that's involved in these recording studios and photographic workshops. Things were so much simpler in the old days when missionaries just used to go out and tell people the Lord loved them...but, you know how some of the old people are. They like to hear of souls saved for the Lord, and people really blessed by the ministry of the Word. There are...well, there are people asking whether the kind of work you're doing is really missionary work in the best sense of the word...."

"I see," Howard said in a colorless tone. "That's why the support is dropping off?"

"Well, you know, that does come into it," admitted the pastor. "I know the old faithfuls aren't always 'with it,' as the young people say, but you can't get away from the fact that they're the ones that give the money. Yes, sir. Without those older people giving, we just couldn't keep anyone on the field."

Between the Lines

"Do you have any suggestion as to what I might do about it?" Howard said through dry lips.

"Well, now, let's take your prayer letters. It sure has been a long time since you told us definitely of people receiving the Lord through your work," said Art, running a hand over his beautifully brushed silver-white hair. "Dorothy was saying just the other day that what people really like to hear is stories like our brother Mike gives us: stories of people really coming to the Lord in their hundreds. I tell you, Howard, that man's support reached a thousand dollars last month."

Howard opened his mouth and shut it again. Of what use would it be to tell Art the truth: that Mike Wilcox had created so much trouble in the Bamor church that eventually the elders had sent a petition to the Mission leader asking that he be sent to another area. Wilcox had come out, with his own support, and announced that he felt a call to evangelize the country around Bamor. Employing his own interpreter, a man unknown to the church elders, he had gone from village to village "preaching the Gospel." Much of what he had said had been misunderstood and he seemed to be totally indifferent to the trouble he was causing; nor was he careful about giving his opinion on various injustices he came across. Eventually the local authorities reported him to the police as a troublemaker and a spy. The ensuing court case was still costing the heads of the mission in Bamor days in court and the writing of endless reports in triplicate. Meanwhile, Mike had cheerfully moved to another area, rejoicing that "the Lord had called him to fresh fields for the winning of souls."

Art, realizing that his words had not been wholly acceptable to Howard, reached over and patted his knee encouragingly. Howard repressed a shudder.

Between the Lines

"I know we can't all be Mikes," Art said, "and we mustn't envy another man's gift, but just think over what I say, Howard. Maybe you could kind of learn to represent your work in a different light or something."

"Yes," Howard said. "Perhaps I could."

"Well," Art stood up. "I'd better get a short rest before the evening service. This visit has been all too short, you know, Howard. All too short. I just can't believe that tomorrow we'll be on the plane for Chicago again. Oh, by the way, the church did want me to leave you a small gift, in appreciation of your hospitality in having Dorothy and me to stay. You know how we've appreciated you and Pat."

He pressed an envelope into Howard's hand and left the room briskly. Howard opened the envelope.

Inside was a check for fifty dollars.

It was about a month after Art and Dorothy had left. Pat came into the house late in the afternoon, having had a longer than usual day at the American school where she taught music. She was surprised to find Howard typing at the dining room table, his usually genial face creased with concentration.

"Hi, Darling," she said. "You're home early."

"Uh-huh," said Howard. Then he looked up. "I was out photographing with Tiapuzi. He had pictures that needed to be taken for an article on death. We spent the time inspecting mortuaries, posing with a skeleton from the medical school, and twining ourselves around graves."

Pat laughed.

Between the Lines

"Must have been a cheerful expedition," she said. "Did you get yourself some supper?"

"No. I...uh...was just working on our prayer letter. I've been meaning to get to it for weeks."

"Good." Pat put her music books down on the table and saw a little pile of letters. "Oh...you stopped by the mail boxes."

"Yes." Howard sounded a little stiff.

"What's the matter?" said Pat. "Is there some bad news in the mail?"

"Just Art and Dorothy's prayer letter telling people about their visit. I left it there for you to see."

"Well, that should be interesting. Wait. I'll just get the supper going and then read it. The children will be home soon."

Pat went into the kitchen and Howard heard her talking to the student who helped them in the house. Then she came back and sat down to read the letter. Howard went on grimly typing until Pat said, "I see what you mean."

Howard stopped. "I didn't know I meant anything."

"But you did." Pat sounded upset. "And I see what it is. Is that the kind of prayer letter you're writing now? With all the bad left out and only glowing reports of the good?"

"I will admit that their letter influenced me in what I'm writing now."

"But, Howard...." Pat got up and came to sit in a chair at the table to face him. "These are lies. Why call them by any other name? Listen to this." She referred to the letter. "'We had a wonderful two days visiting the brethren at Bamor. How encouraging it was to see the church filled with new converts and to hear them thank us for sending them missionaries to tell them the good news. It did our hearts good to hear the joyous singing of men and women rejoicing in the Savior, and to see the happy spirit in the hospital which your giving brought into existence.' It makes me sick!"

"It's just another way of looking at things," Howard said. "That's what the people at home want to hear. So Art writes it that way."

"But it's not true!"

"So how do you think he should have written? Did you want him to tell them that half the hospital workers are out on strike because their pay is too little; that the church in Bamor has been split down the middle by tribalism and selfishness; that 'brother Mike's' evangelism has brought on the Mission the charge of spying? What kind of support do you think that would have brought us?"

Pat was silent.

Howard looked down at his typewriter. "I didn't share with you all that Art told me on that last day," he said. "He virtually said that unless I could produce a few statistics of souls saved through my ministry, the support would continue to drop."

"So what are you writing?"

Howard ripped the almost finished letter from the machine and gave it to her. He then shut the machine and began to clear the table, as the student came in to set the table for supper.

Pat read the letter. It began, "We praise the Lord for the twelve new believers baptized in the church last Sunday. What joy it has been to see them come to the Lord and to know that we, and you at home, have a share in this harvest...." She stopped.

"Howard, did you know any of those baptized?"

Between the Lines

"Not personally, no. I knew some by name."

"And how much were you involved in their conversion or their instruction before baptism?"

"I don't know. They may easily have been influenced by the magazine or the filmstrips we produce."

Pat skimmed through the rest of the letter and put it down.

"Howard, don't do it," she said. "It isn't worth it."

"I'm just being practical. Others do it. Why shouldn't we? I haven't made any false claims in that letter. Let the implications take care of themselves. This is the last prayer letter we have to send before furlough. Don't you realize that our reception, our furlough housing, pay, supplies, will depend on the spirit in which the church receives us? They want that. Let them have it."

"I just don't see how God can bless us financially, or in any other way, if we build our support on lies."

"It's not lies," Howard said stubbornly. "It's just talking about different things in our prayer letter. It isn't you that has to go and explain to the school director that we can't clear that debt before we go home. I believe in my ministry, Pat, and I want to stay in it. If this is the only way I can, then I'll take it.

"Anyway, the Lord sure isn't blessing us financially as it is. If anyone questions me closely about my work I'll tell them the truth: that it's in graphics, print and photography. But I'm still going to send this letter!"

Early in January, Howard was in his office with his assistant, preparing a camera-ready mechanical for the printer, when Tiapuzi, the young editor of the chief Christian publication in the city, came in. They were old friends and when the greetings had been exchanged,

Tiapuzi said, "I hear your time for leave has come round.'

"Yes," Howard said. "We leave in February."

"Until...?"

"Until our church decides to send us back," Howard said in a carefully expressionless voice. "That partly depends on what the church here decides it wants."

"There's no doubt we want you back, Howard," Tiapuzi said, smiling at him. "You know the value of what you're doing for us."

Howard flushed a little.

"Thanks for saying that, Tiapuzi," he said. "I appreciate it; but you know missionaries should only stay until nationals are ready to take on their jobs. I don't want to stay around too long. You could find nationals to manage here now."

"Not yet, Brother," Tiapuzi said firmly. "That's partly what I wanted to see you about. You know you've been wanting to teach a course in design and photography for years. Well, I have the students for you."

"What do you mean?" Howard looked up.

"There are two young men available in June who want to work in design and photography. One of them I expect to take on in a year's time as Art Editor for the magazine. The church has agreed to let them study under you for one year, beginning in September. September is about when you'd return. Right?"

"That would be great." Howard's earnest face glowed with pleasure. "I really have wanted opportunities to train others. But...." His face fell.

"But?" prompted Tiapuzi.

"Maybe...our church won't send us back. You know the giving hasn't been all it might be...we've found it rather difficult. They're...they're not used to thinking of people like me as missionaries."

"So who do they think of as missionaries?" said Tiapuzi, surprised.

"Well...." Howard said reluctantly. "I think some of them see the work of a missionary as primarily evangelism...."

Tiapuzi's face hardened. "Like Mr. Wilcox, I suppose," he said.

Howard said nothing.

Tiapuzi got up. "Howard, we hear the Western church always talking about helping us," he said. "But do they have to tell us where we need the help, or can they believe we might know our needs better than they do?"

"I'll try and explain to them," said Howard unhappily.

But when they were on leave it was much more difficult than Howard had imagined. For one thing he had to confess to the debt he still owed the American school, and for another, the pastor had taken him aside when they'd got home and said, "You know, Howard, that last prayer letter of yours helped matters so much. The elders were delighted. We really prayed for those twelve brethren you mentioned. I hope you've brought slides of the baptism and everything."

Howard felt Pat at his elbow. He had replied in a hollow voice, "Oh yes, Pastor. We've got some great slides."

For the first three weeks they had stayed with Pat's folks while the Church Missionary Committee decided on their housing. Howard had given two talks: one during the evening service and one to the ladies'

Between the Lines

missionary circle. For the evening service he had dug out some old slides of their early days as missionaries in a country area: women with water pots, overloaded donkeys, children in a small Sunday school, and a baptism in a river. Then he commented that the work of the Gospel was still going on, and showed slides of the recent baptism in the city church to which he and Pat belonged. The people had seemed to receive it all right but he'd had to face embarrassing questions afterwards like, "Did that young boy on the left have his parents' permission to be baptized?" or, "How long was it from the time most of them first heard the Gospel to the time they were baptized?"

Howard, who had only the sketchiest knowledge of the twelve concerned, was agonizingly aware of Pat at his elbow as he stammered out answers which were as general as he could make them. He heard Pat say to one lady, "I'm teaching most of the day. I really have very little to do with Howard's work," and knew he was forcing her, too, to be part of his dishonesty.

Pat hadn't come to the ladies' missionary circle, pleading a headache, and Howard really excelled himself with a story of a little boy called Roen, whom he and Pat had found friendless and hungry in the street and sent to school with a suit of new clothes. He was especially good about the time the little lad woke his dormitory by singing "Jesus Loves Me" in his sleep. The story was based on truth. It was true that Pat and he had sent the child to a school run for orphans by another mission. What he didn't say was that Roen had been a thoroughly unsatisfactory student. He had run away from school several times and had had to be searched for and brought back. He had never shown the slightest interest in Christianity, and the story about singing "Jesus Loves Me" in his sleep really happened to another student. Howard, however, without ever actually stating it, allowed the ladies to picture Roen as a little lamb, grateful to be gathered into the Lord's flock. He tried not to feel badly about the tears he saw on one or two faces as he drew to a sentimental close. His honorarium at the end of the meeting was nearly a hundred dollars.

That evening Pat said to him, "I heard that the only house they can give us to live in is in Harlow."

"Harlow?" Howard was startled. "That's a little way from the church."

"Does that worry you?"

"Well...uh...yes. After all, the whole point of furlough is for the supporting church to get to know us again and...." his voice trailed off. He sat down suddenly and said, "Pat, thanks for not telling me what you've thought about all this. I'm sorry. I really am."

"But you're going to go right on doing it?"

"I want to get back to Africa. I believe in what I'm doing and I want to go on doing it."

"Don't let's go over it again now." Pat got up to get them an evening drink. "Let's see what Harlow has to offer in the way of a church."

"But...surely...we'll have to come over here to church?" Howard said, surprised.

"Why? It would be much more sensible to get into a church there...easier on all counts, especially since no-one's thought to provide us with a car."

"But…I'm sure anyone in the church would come over and get us."

"Howard," Pat said slowly, "I've been wondering why we stay with a church that demands we fit exactly into their conception of a missionary. Why can't we find one that is ready to support us for what we are?"

Howard stared at her. "But we owe everything to this church," he said. "Why, even the rent of the house we'll be living in will be paid by them."

"We're due six months' paid leave," Pat said. "After that, if the worst comes to the worst, I could get a teaching job and you could start looking for something else. We're not bound to this church, Howard. We can look around for other support."

She went into the kitchen, and Howard looked after her worriedly.

Spring passed on into sweltering summer. It was late June when Dorothy came into Art's study looking rather flustered.

"It's Pastor West to see you, Dear. From the Harlow church. He says he has an appointment."

"Yes, that's right, Dorothy. I forgot to mention it to you."

Art got up, brushing a speck of dust from his sleeve. "Just ask him to come in."

He knew Alec West by repute as one of the pastors attached to Christ's Community Church in Harlow; a church which had, in the last ten years, been growing rapidly.

"Well, Pastor West," he said as the younger man entered. "This is an unexpected pleasure. I don't know that I've ever had a chance to shake you by the hand, though I've wanted to often enough."

West was a large, kindly-looking man, in his early forties, with a powerful nose and thinning fair hair. He greeted Art pleasantly, accepting the offer of coffee and chatting for a few minutes about his church and the work they had recently initiated among the mentally handicapped. Presently he introduced the object of his call.

Between the Lines

"It's about Howard and Pat Fraser," he said. "They've been living near our church, as you know, and we've been seeing them quite often."

"Well, I'm glad to hear that," Art said. "I realize it's a little far for them to come here every Sunday, though of course we do like to see plenty of our missionaries when they're on leave. They're all very precious to us, Pastor West. Very precious. Howard has been able to share some very lovely things with us...yes, some very sweet things. The ladies' missionary circle has been particularly impressed. Why, just the other day a lady pressed a gift into my hand for some of the new converts Howard has been telling us about."

"And when is it they return to Africa?" inquired West.

Art appeared embarrassed.

"Well, Brother West...between you and me, there is some question about that. You see Howard and Pat—I'm sure they won't mind my sharing this with you—landed here with quite a debt and some of the elders did wonder if...well, if there had been some extravagance there...."

"I thought it was for their children's school fees," West said without emotion.

"Well...yes, it was," admitted Art, "but there was also the question of Howard's work. He works in an office, you know...in the city, and it seems it has little to do with what we call...uh...grassroots missionary service. People around here, you see, do like to know that the true Gospel is being preached to the heathen."

"But don't you think Howard's work is worthwhile?" asked West.

"Yes, yes, of course. No one doubts that," said Art hurriedly. "I was over there at Thanksgiving you know, so I had a good chance to see things for myself. Of course it's worthwhile; it's just that...well, you know how it is, we have to have priorities in all church giving."

"I see," West said thoughtfully. "So there is some question as to whether your church will recommend their return?"

"Some question, yes," Art said. "I wouldn't put it stronger than that at the moment."

"Hmm." West finished his coffee and set the cup down carefully. "Let me be frank with you, Pastor Johnson. Our church in Harlow, as you may have heard, is growing fast. The congregation—that is, the Bible class—to which Howard and Pat temporarily belong, have been praying for some time that the Lord would show them how they can become more deeply involved in mission work. They've become very interested in what Howard is doing in audiovisuals, especially in this new opportunity he has to teach the nationals design and photography. We wondered if you'd allow us to help towards their support."

Art looked startled. This was something he had not expected.

"Well," he said. "That's very generous of you, Pastor West. Very generous. I'm sure in many ways it would be a great relief to our missionary budget if you could assist us. We...uh...have the system where the money that comes in for general missionary use is divided equally among our missionaries...except for personal gifts, of course...That is, if we do send the Frasers back."

"Our principle is that the church contracts to send the missionary a certain sum each month," West said. "My thought was that you would continue to give whatever came in and we would make it up each month to the stated sum. We feel it helps the missionary to plan his own way if he knows what he can expect each month."

"I expect our elders would agree to that. Of course you would want to discuss with Howard just what his work is...."

"Excuse me, Brother," West said quietly but firmly. "We have one stipulation to make over this. We don't feel we should tell Howard what work we want him to do. We will expect nothing from him or his family except that they follow the Lord's leading day by day in whatever work He leads them into. If God leads them to spend the day digging ditches for Him, that's OK with us. We want to support them as a brother and sister in Christ who are serving the national church. In any way."

"I see." Art looked steadily at West. "Howard has clearly been...sharing some things with you."

"Yes." Alec West returned the look. "He will, I know, want to discuss them with you too. I just wanted to speak to you first and tell you that we have confidence in Howard and Pat, and if your church feels at any time that you do not wish to support them, we are prepared to support them fully."

The evening valedictory sermon that Howard Fraser preached in his home church on August 20 was a point of discussion in the congregation for years. Both he and Pat were on the platform with a somewhat uncomfortable-looking Art. Howard's face was a little pale as he stepped forward to speak, but his voice was steady. For about ten minutes he spoke from a biblical text about the unity of the church of God. Then he gently closed the Bible and looked down at the congregation.

Between the Lines

"Before I close, tonight," he said, "I have a confession that I need to make publicly, before you all."

People looked up. There was a complete and wondering silence in the church.

"I have to tell you," continued Howard firmly, "that in the prayer letter I wrote to you before coming on leave, and in the addresses I gave to you when I first came home, I lied to you. I have allowed you to think my work is in winning people for the Lord in our church and in building them up to strength in Christ. It is true that, just before we came home, twelve men and women were baptized into that church. It is not true that my work concerns them in any way. Most of the Africans I meet have been Christians for many years; I am not involved in direct evangelism and have not been for over four years."

Every eye was on him. Some people were frowning a little.

"You have the right to know why I lied," said Howard slowly. "It was because I had observed that you wished to give your money to the work of—I use your words—winning souls for Jesus. It seemed to me that if I told you my work had continued to be in a city office with a few African Christians, you would no longer support me. I should have known that the continuance of my work does not depend on you, but on God. It is my own weakness and lack of faith that I speak of. I ask your forgiveness that I showed it in this way."

For the first time his voice faltered, but he continued steadily, "But I would not be true to the Spirit testifying within me if I did not also speak of your mistake. Many of you see missionary work as it was fifty years ago: preaching to the uneducated heathen, baptizing believers, building up tiny churches in the African bush. But it is the very fact that such work was done fifty years ago that means there are churches today that need care and teaching in all different facets of modern life. Many of the churches have their own evangelists, able to reach the people far better than foreigners ever will. They ask now for teachers, technicians, specialists in agriculture, literacy, radio broadcasting: people who can help them most quickly to take their place in modern Africa. Are you not willing to support them as once you supported evangelists?"

Art stirred restlessly and Howard took out his handkerchief and wiped his forehead. He was beginning to sweat under the hot lights.

"This isn't to say there are not places on the earth where pioneer evangelists are needed. But it is to say that if you send missionaries to parts of Africa where the national church is growing and healthy, you must not expect them to be involved in direct evangelism, unless that is the gift God has given them.

"Don't equate the gift of missionary with the gift of evangelist. A missionary, as I see him, is one specially gifted to use his abilities in another country. A teacher will teach, a farmer will farm, a writer will write. Of course we are all witnesses to Christ and our lives must always testify to the grace of God; we will take gladly, joyfully, any opportunity the Lord gives us to lead another man to Christ. But just as you do not ask an artist to evaluate his work in terms of the houses he has built, so you must not judge every missionary's work by the number of souls he has won.

"I believe in my work. Secular literature, much of it communist-inspired, is flooding the country and, beside it, Christian literature looks dull and unattractive. I can help the African Christian to illustrate his work in a way that will cause a man to look again, to buy it. Who knows how many are brought to Christ in that way? I can show young men with little knowledge of photography how to take pictures that are instantly understood, that carry in themselves a powerful message of need, or joy, or unhappiness. This is what the African church is asking me to do; it is what I enjoy doing...but it does not seem to be the kind of work you want to support."

Howard paused, trying to keep the bitterness from his tone, knowing that to sound bitter would only take away from the truths he was trying to explain. He went on more gently.

"Why do you give to Christian missionary work? To earn something? To feel good? To feel you have 'bought' some souls for Jesus through the missionary's work? Is the missionary you support your employee, there to do your will because your money supports him? No. The money you give is not yours, but God's; you give to Him. The missionary you give to is God's servant, not yours; he is responsible first to God. Once you have decided that a member of your congregation has the missionary gift and is truly called by God, then send him out with your blessing and your prayers that he will find the daily pathway that the Lord intends him to walk on. Only then will missionaries begin to be honest with you.

"I am not the only missionary who has been unable to speak of the things nearest my heart. What money can we expect if we tell you that our biggest problem, and the one we most need prayer for, is our bad relationships with the national church? What would be your reaction if I told you I chiefly need money for a more modern type of developing-tank?

Between the Lines

"So instead of being honest, we search out and elaborate dramatic stories of men and women coming to Christ. If we can stir you to tears we can be sure of over a hundred dollars at the end of a meeting. Friends, brothers and sisters in Christ, is that really the type of missionary you want to support? Do you want us to dramatize incidents we have all but forgotten? Do you really want to hear only the bright side of things? Or do you want to support men and women struggling to follow Christ as you are, but willing to do it in exile from their own country, in a new culture, using another language, looking to you for encouragement and help?"

Howard was coming to an end. He began to gather the papers in front of him.

"So forgive me for lying to you. None of us is perfect, but in the Body of Christ we have a right to expect from each other love and forgiveness and understanding. That is what I am asking from you tonight."

He went back to his chair. Art, looking rather white around the mouth, came forward and announced the last hymn.

Three things stood out to Howard following that service. Hearing one woman say to another, "Well! And that's the man we've been supporting!" Hearing Dorothy say to Pat, "My dear, that must have been embarrassing for you to sit through," and Pat's reply: "I've never been prouder of any address Howard has given." And the grip of a young man who introduced himself as a college professor, who said, "At last I've heard a missionary be honest. Congratulations, Sir, and if you tell me just how to go about it, I will be glad to pledge support to you and your wife."

Howard went down the steps of the church, shaking hands automatically with those who stood to greet him, to find friends from the Harlow Bible Class had called to take them home.

Chapter 8
The Triangle Again

Margaret wiped the sweat from her forehead with the back of a floury hand and tried to push back a strand of hair that was getting into her eyes. The outside kitchen was built of stone, and the combination of the fierce heat of the African afternoon and the wood-burning stove made the atmosphere unbearably hot and sticky. She usually did any cooking there was to do early, but mid-way through the morning she had found that the meat bought yesterday had gone bad and so had decided to have a cheese-and-onion pie for supper. Jenny would be coming off an all-day bus and would need something more substantial than scrambled eggs. Margaret's little servant, Birhan, was there helping her, but she could not trust her to make pastry; she kneaded it as if it were bread, and Julian tended to grumble at the biscuit-crust result.

Outside, along the main road from the west which ran past their compound, she heard the hooter of the bus from the city announcing its arrival in their small, provincial town. The study door slammed outside and she heard her husband's voice.

The Triangle Again

"Hey, you kids! If you want to come with me to meet Aunt Jenny, you must come right away. The bus is early."

She heard the excited voices of the children as they piled into the car, and glanced out of the kitchen to see the little blue Volkswagen chug out in a cloud of dust, to follow the bus to the marketplace where it would unload its passengers. She reckoned she had about twenty minutes to get ready for Jenny's arrival. She finished the pie, checked the oven heat and turned to explain for the fiftieth time to Birhan how to keep the temperature of the oven at medium heat by feeding in wood slowly.

A shadow fell in the bright doorway.

"Mrs. Margaret?" It was Selas, the cook from the town, who had been hired for the duration of the two-month Bible course. "I need another pan to make the stew for dinner."

"But surely that big one is enough for thirty students," Margaret said, surprised. "We managed last year."

"But some of the students can't eat red pepper, and they've asked me to prepare some stew without pepper in it," the woman explained.

Margaret sighed. The students got more sophisticated each year. A year or two ago they were so excited at getting three free meals a day out of the Mission that they had never complained about the food. Now, they even wanted a special diet.

"Well...I'll come and see if I can find one in the school equipment shed," Margaret said, unhooking the key from its nail in the kitchen, and stepping out into the fierce glare of the sun and the crackling grass of the drought-held compound. Her head ached a little.

The Triangle Again

Suddenly, a crying child erupted from some bushes and hurled itself at Margaret, clutching her skirt with two dirty hands.

"Mummy, Daddy's gone without me and he *promised* I could go to the market to meet Aunt Jenny and it was my turn to ride in the front seat!" wailed little seven-year-old Ruth.

"Never mind, Darling," Margaret said, absent-mindedly detaching the grimy hands. "You can go next time. Come and help Mama Selas and me look for another pan in the shed."

Ruth hung on her hand, whining, "I'm too hot. Can't we play at the swimming pool?"

"You know we can't until the rains come, Ruthie," said Margaret, trying to be patient. "And where are your shoes? You know I asked you to wear them to stop yourself getting jiggers."

"I hate shoes," Ruth said fretfully, and Margaret tried to control a sharp answer. The heat was trying for the children especially.

She opened the shed and eventually, after a long hunt, they unearthed an old cooking-pot that would do until they could get to the market on Saturday and buy another. Walking back to the house, Margaret smelt the pie burning and saw the Volkswagen turn in at the drive. She would have to receive Jenny as she was. The two older children tumbled out of it, sucking lollipops. They saw Ruth and yelled at her, "Where'd you go, Ruthie? Daddy bought us lollipops while we waited for Aunt Jenny to get off the bus!"

"Well, I hope you brought Ruthie one!" Margaret said sharply, but they hadn't, and under this fresh sense of injustice Ruth started to cry again. Margaret saw

The Triangle Again

Birhan slinking towards the kitchen from the servants' quarters.

"Birhan, that pie is burning!" she called sharply. "I thought I told you not to pile wood on the stove!"

It was into this scene of temper and tears that Jenny Wright stepped that hot August afternoon.

Jenny was in her first term as a missionary. She was twenty-six: long-legged, smooth-skinned, her long, dark hair drawn back from her face by a green chiffon scarf. Somehow, as Margaret had known she would, she managed to look as if she had just stepped from a British Airways jet rather than from a noisy, smelly bus on which she had traveled all day.

Julian, whose lean body and freckled skin also never seemed affected by the heat, had lifted her case from the boot of the car. He glanced indifferently at the squabbling children and said, "Come into the house, Jenny, and I'll find you something cool to drink."

"In a minute," Jenny said and came up to Margaret to greet her, kissing her lightly on the cheek.

"I can't shake hands with you." Margaret held out her hands and tried to smile. "I've just been searching for something in the equipment shed. But it's good to see you, Jenny. Don't stand in the sun. Go in with Julian and I'll bring you a drink."

She felt agonizingly the contrast between her shapeless, locally-made cotton dress and flip-flop sandals, and Jenny's attractive non-iron dress and white shoes, and she longed to get inside and change.

"Mummy, I want a *lollipop!*" Ruth screamed.

"Ruth, if you don't stop that noise, you'll get a good slap!" said Julian, annoyed at the confusion.

The Triangle Again

"Well, it was your fault for not waiting for her this afternoon," Margaret could not help saying. "She was looking forward to the trip."

Julian looked a little ashamed and ruffled Ruth's hair. "Sorry, kiddo," he said. "Come inside and I'll find something else for you."

Ruth consented to be led into the house and Jenny followed them.

Margaret glanced into the kitchen, at the blazing stove and the burnt pie, and tried to pretend to herself that it didn't matter. They would have to open a tin of tuna fish. She went into the living-room and opened the refrigerator, which they had switched on for the day in honor of Jenny's coming—paraffin was too expensive to keep it running all the time—and took out a jug of lime juice. Julian was sitting alone while Jenny was freshening up in the bathroom.

"You look all in, Margaret," Julian said, looking at her critically. "You really should let Birhan do more for you."

"He's contrasting me with her already!" thought Margaret to herself with a surge of panic, but she replied equably. "Well, I had to get most of the students settled into their dormitories. I'll be fine when I've had a chance to wash and change. Mama Selas came and wanted another pan because...." But Julian interrupted her. He rarely took an interest in domestic matters.

"Did you ask the teachers to meet us tonight?" he asked. "We really must get down to finalizing the program."

"I called them for eight," Margaret answered, trying not to mind that the "us" were now Julian and Jenny, who would be the main teachers in the forthcoming Bible school.

The Triangle Again

"Mummy! We want drinks!" The two boys were stampeding into the living-room.

"You won't get anything if you ask for it like that!" Julian said sharply. "Go to the bathroom and wash your faces and hands, and then come and sit down properly!"

Margaret wondered if she would ever get to the bathroom. Jenny reappeared, accepted the drink gratefully and said, "It's great to be here, Margaret. I've really been looking forward to it."

"It's good you could come," Margaret answered quietly. "I'm sorry we're in the middle of such a drought, but we've been saving you enough water for a bath tonight."

"That's something I would love," agreed Jenny. "Those buses aren't the cleanest way to travel!"

The boys came back subdued and certainly cleaner, and Julian and Jenny started to discuss the coming classes. Margaret at last got to the bathroom and, carefully ladelling water into a bowl, began to wash off the flour and dust. She scowled at her face in the mirror, large and red with exertion and exposure, and tried to put on a little make-up; but it was unsuccessful. The make-up base and powder had been bought in England for her complexion before the sun had changed its color, and it looked like a dusting of flour on a healthy apple. She combed her hair and tried to make it neater, put on a fresh dress that she had to admit was getting a trifle tight for her, and squeezed her spread feet into her one pair of English shoes. The result did not excite her, but it was better. Ten minutes later her hands were grimy and smudged with oil from her effort to get an old pressure-lamp working for the students in their dining room.

When she had finally got the lamp working, she lit their own and took it into the living room, only to find

The Triangle Again

that Julian and Jenny had moved across to Julian's study, a little hut unattached to the main house. Peering through the twilight she saw a light go on over there, and moved uncomfortably in the tight shoes to the kitchen to open the tin of tuna fish. If Julian was to have the teachers' meeting at eight, he would want his meal before seven-thirty, their usual time. Tears pricked behind her eyelids. For months she had refused to face up to the fact that things were not right between her and Julian, and the coming of a young and attractive woman was obviously going to be a threat to her in a way she would not have believed possible a year ago.

At a quarter to seven Margaret sent Birhan across to the study to call them to supper. It was nearly dark. She would have much preferred to give the children their meal earlier, but having the meal early themselves made that impossible. Ruth, comforted by a tube of Smarties, was less fractious than sometimes, and the boys, David and Tim, were eagerly at the table.

"Oh not tuna *again*, Mum!"

"Well, if you don't like it, you can leave it," said Margaret, firmly dishing it out with a practiced hand and smiling a welcome at Jenny. "There's a bowl in the kitchen for hand washing, Jenny. I'm afraid we just can't afford fresh water for everyone."

"That's fine," Jenny disappeared into the kitchen and presently they were all seated around the table, while Julian cut the bread rapidly and the children argued over how many of the little, bitter tomatoes each could have.

"You must tell us all the news from headquarters, Jenny," said Margaret cheerfully, when grace had been said. "Is Barbara better?"

The Triangle Again

"Dad, Samuel pinched our ball this morning an' we never got it back," David said suddenly, giving up on the tomatoes.

"David, your mother was speaking to Auntie Jenny," Julian said severely. "Don't interrupt."

"But, Dad...."

"Be quiet, David!"

Why was it, Margaret thought despairingly, that the children were always so badly behaved when they had guests? They didn't have enough guests really. Perhaps it was that the children weren't accustomed to sharing their parents' attention with anyone else.

Jenny pretended she had not heard the altercation and chatted pleasantly about things in the city. Margaret, listening and asking the occasional question about one person or another, was chiefly aware of Julian's alert, interested face and bright manner. When had he looked like that, or behaved like that, talking to her, she thought. She saw to everyone's needs and tried to keep the children as quiet as possible, but she saw Julian's eyes flicker sometimes to the front of Jenny's dress, which though modestly cut, outlined her young breasts attractively. Once, when he passed Jenny the butter she saw his hand brush lightly against her arm.

"Don't take such big mouthfuls," she said sharply to Tim.

After supper, Julian got out the big chart of the Bible School time-table and spread it on the table. He began to explain it to Jenny, while Margaret helped Birhan clear away and wash up.

"I've arranged for you to take a short devotional with the girl students three days a week at eleven," Julian was saying.

Jenny looked alarmed.

The Triangle Again

"I hope my language is up to it," she said. "I've only prepared for the three courses."

"You'll manage fine," Julian said encouragingly, smiling at her.

"I'm sure someone else could do it better," Jenny protested. "Couldn't Margaret?"

"Oh, Margaret's language has never really progressed beyond that of the kitchen," said Julian, throwing a casual, "Has it, Dear?" over his shoulder at Margaret putting the cutlery away. "Anyway, she likes to be left free while the children are at home from school. I'm sure you can manage, Jenny. I took you for your first language exam, remember?'

She acknowledged it with a smile.

Julian, consulting something at the top left-hand of the paper, leant against her, his forearm lightly touching her smooth, bare arm. Jenny got up.

"Let me help you, Margaret," she said, "That was a lovely tuna salad."

Was she aware of Julian's glances? wondered Margaret, accepting the offer of help. Rather grudgingly, watching her, she thought probably not. She knew something of Jenny's strict evangelical background as the only daughter of a well-known Bible teacher in England and the product of a famous Christian school. She had heard that she was a conscientious missionary, deeply concerned with the Lord and her work for Him. As yet the sheer battle for spiritual survival as a missionary had not touched her.

At eight, one of the teachers came to call Julian and Jenny, and they went off together. Margaret applied herself to getting Ruth into bed.

They came back late from the meeting and then Julian spent a long time talking to Jenny in the living

The Triangle Again

room. Margaret, in bed, was aware of the light through the crack of the door, and thought how Julian usually grumbled at late nights wasting the precious paraffin supply. She heard the low tone of their voices: Jenny's pleasant voice and Julian's sudden bark of laughter, hushed because he remembered she was in the next room.

Finally, he said goodnight to Jenny and the strong light disappeared. Julian brought a small oil lamp into their bedroom.

"Meeting go well?" she said.

He started: guiltily, she thought.

"Yes, I think so," he said, sitting down on the bed to take his shoes off. "It finished some time ago actually. I was just clearing up some points with Jenny."

"You must have enjoyed that," said Margaret before she could stop herself.

He turned around to look at her.

"What does that mean?"

"Well, you obviously enjoy her company," said Margaret, trying to speak lightly. "You haven't taken your eyes off her since she arrived."

Julian thrust his feet into flip-flops and stood up abruptly to take his shirt off. "You're being ridiculous," he said shortly. "She's just a colleague who needs to be given confidence in the job she's being asked to do. It's all new to her here, you know."

"Well, you certainly must be giving her confidence as a woman," Margaret said spitefully.

"I don't know what you mean, Margaret, and I'm not sure I want to," said Julian, putting on a dressing gown. "And I want to get to the bathroom before Jenny starts having her bath."

The Triangle Again

"Well, let me tell you what I mean," Margaret said, sitting up suddenly. "I've seen the way you look at her. When was the last time you looked at me like that?"

"Margaret," Julian tried to be patient. "This isn't the moment. I'm tired out...we'll talk about whatever it is that's upset you tomorrow...."

"You're always tired out," Margaret said, tearful now. "When did you last make love to me, tell me that? You don't even see me as a woman anymore...."

"Oh, for God's sake!" Julian said exasperatedly. "How many people want to make love every night in a temperature of ninety-six? It's news to me that you care that much about that side of things, anyway. Go to sleep!"

But Margaret had begun now and could not stop. It came spilling out of her: all the bitterness, the hurt, the loneliness....

"I would care about 'that side of things,' as you call it, if you did," she said. "But you don't! You don't even try to share anything with me anymore. You aren't interested in how I spend my day and the problems I might have, and you tell me practically nothing about what you're doing. What kind of a marriage is that?"

"Keep your voice down," Julian said furiously. "If you must have a scene at midnight when we're both tired out, do you want Jenny to hear every word?"

"Do you know what the woodman said to me this evening?" Margaret demanded, but in a quieter tone. "He said 'It's good your son have woman now!' He thought you were my son!"

"He's new to the place: an ignorant man who's probably never seen white people before," Julian said, trying to calm her. "Are you going to be upset by the chance remark of a country African? Look, Margaret, I am going to the bathroom...."

The Triangle Again

He moved towards the door, only to realize that Jenny had been just before him. He heard the door close and water being poured out of buckets.

"Damn!" he said. "Now I'll have to wait until she finishes."

"You'd better go in there with her," Margaret said viciously. "She'd look even better naked!"

She was sorry immediately. Julian sat down wearily on the bed.

"Do you have to make remarks like that?" he said.

"I'm...sorry," she said in a muffled voice. "I don't know what's come over me."

"It's OK. It's the drought, I expect. It's trying on us all," he said tiredly. Then, after a pause, "Perhaps you're right. We are kind of losing touch. It's probably my fault."

The quiet statement frightened her more than his anger had.

"Well...we can get back into touch again, can't we?" she asked timidly.

"I don't know." He sounded almost as if he was talking to himself. "I have a feeling that...sometimes people allow themselves to get...so far apart that they never do...really get together again...."

She tried to answer and failed. She lay down again, turning away from him. Hot, bitter tears squeezed themselves out from under her eyelids. She'd been a fool: a jealous fool.

It was certain that their talk, to which they did not refer again, had not helped matters. The way the old African had thought Margaret to be his mother stuck and rankled with Julian, despite his efforts to put it out of his mind. He had realized early in his married life that intellectually and creatively Margaret was not his

The Triangle Again

equal, but he had, on the whole, accepted her for what she was: pleasant, undemanding, a good mother of his children and someone who kept his home going for him. He had not thought much about her appearance, but now, he began to notice just how plain, over-weight and badly-dressed she was, and how dull her conversation. For Jenny was with him daily.

He would, in any case, have admired Jenny's obvious absorption in her work, for he himself had high professional standards, but he began to find it difficult not to think also of her physical attractions. He noticed things about her in the evenings when she sat at the dining room table correcting papers: her slim waist, the way her hair swung forward to reveal her slender neck, how the paleness of her inside forearm merged with the suntan of her arm. He found, when they were with the students, that he knew at once if she had come into the room and he had to school himself not to look at her too often.

And Margaret watched them both, still not certain that Jenny was aware of the situation in her anxiety to do the Bible teaching well in the still-unfamiliar language. There was no-one to whom Margaret could turn, no friend to sympathize with her, no pastor to give wise counsel. Remembering from a distant past the instructions of women's magazines to keep attractive for your husband, she spent hours wondering what to do about her appearance. But they had been away from England too long. The dresses she had brought with her were either worn out by now or too tight. What she wore now had been made by local tailors who, in their desire to have a lot of cloth left over that they could re-sell, made dresses as tight as possible. Such dresses, with large patterns and bright colors, did not flatter her.

The Triangle Again

She had no suitable make-up. The long drought had made her hair dry and wispy, and, though she could get cheap shampoos in the town, no-one had ever heard of conditioners. She felt defeated before she had begun. She prayed desperately for wisdom, for understanding, for forgiveness for both herself and Julian.

Mid-way through the course it was the custom to take the students studying methods of evangelism to a small village called Dneifan, where the mission had once had a Bible school. A long weekend was spent there, most of it in visiting the out-lying areas. About three or four women were involved, and therefore Julian had told Jenny he expected her to go with them. At supper, a few days before they were due to go, Julian said to Margaret, "Jenny is bringing a women's team to Dneifan at the weekend, so we'll need both land rovers and the Volkswagen. Can you manage without transport over the weekend?"

"Of course," said Margaret calmly.

The children broke in excitedly.

"Daddy, are you going to Dneifan? Can we come too?"

"Daddy…you promised we could come next time!"

"There's no room this time," Julian said. "There's only just enough room for the students. I'll take you another weekend."

"You always say that," Tim said sulkily, "and we never go!"

"That'll do, Tim," Julian said coldly.

Three days later the two land rovers and the Volkswagen set off. Julian had told Jenny to get into the front seat of the one he was driving. He kissed Margaret goodbye perfunctorily, waved to the other vehicles to precede him, and they left.

The Triangle Again

The students welcomed the change from the classroom and, when they got to Dneifan, threw themselves into making the old Bible school buildings habitable for the weekend. They started the visiting program almost immediately on the Saturday and had hilarious sessions on Saturday and Sunday evenings discussing the activities of the day. It seemed almost a holiday camp atmosphere at times and both Julian and Jenny enjoyed the outdoor life and the relaxation from study.

They had planned to leave on Monday afternoon and, as they began to load up the vehicles, Julian glanced around.

"Where's Miss Jenny?" he asked.

"She went to the cliff edge," they told him. "Shall we go and tell her we're ready to go?"

Julian lifted a kitbag into the back of the land rover and said, as casually as he could, "No...I'll go along and fetch her. Get the cars loaded. I'll be right back."

His heart beating suddenly fast, he walked along the dried earth track through the eucalyptus trees towards the cliff. The cliff edge had been a favorite spot for all of them during the weekend when they had time off. You reached it through the closely-growing trees and suddenly found yourself on a gently sloping field which ended at a two-thousand-foot drop to the lowlands below. It was said, on a good day, that you could see over a hundred miles. Jenny had probably gone there for a last look at the view...it would be a very new type of country for her.

He hoped very much that she had come alone, and then, as he came out of the trees, he saw her standing, looking out over the great silent plains of the lowlands. He approached quietly, but the ground was stony and

The Triangle Again

his foot set a small rock rolling. She turned to see him. Her first thought was that she had kept them waiting.

"Oh...Julian!" She turned to hurry towards him. "Are you ready to go? I had to come and see the view just once more."

In her haste she slipped. Julian took her arm to steady her.

"Thanks." She laughed a little awkwardly and tried to draw away from him, but instead he tightened his grip, turning her gently to face him, his other hand on her arm.

"Don't be in such a hurry to go, Jenny." He said quietly. "They won't be ready for a while."

She looked up, taken by surprise, and Julian saw her face change as she looked at him and read his look correctly. She stood quite still, color first leaving her face and then flooding back. Then she said jerkily, "Let me go, Julian."

"Are you sure you want me to?" he said gently, smiling down at her.

She pulled herself away and they stood facing each other on the stone-covered earth. She made an effort to speak normally.

"I'm sure the others must be ready to go. We'd better go back."

He came nearer her. "I'm telling you they're not ready yet, Jenny," he said. "Forget them. Can't we enjoy being alone together: just for once?"

"Don't touch me."

She moved away again and then glanced, in sudden alarm, around her, as if realizing their isolation for the first time. Julian interpreted her look and was hurt.

"For heaven's sake, Jenny," he said. "I'm not going to harm you. I won't even touch you again if it upsets you

The Triangle Again

so much. But I thought you knew what I've come to feel about you."

"You're married," Jenny said in a small voice. Her flush had died. She looked white and strained. "I've always thought of you as Margaret's husband. Nothing else."

He saw it was true.

"I'm a man too, Jenny," he said, "and you're a woman. It's true I'm Margaret's husband but...but a man needs other friends in his life...particularly when his wife can't give him the love he needs."

She was staring at him, as if castles of innocence and naivety were crumbling around her, as indeed they were.

"You're a missionary...my senior missionary. I never thought of you as anything else. I've been guided by you. I didn't think...a missionary couple would...be like others...."

Julian's mouth twisted rather bitterly.

"Well, learn differently now," he said. "Missionaries aren't saints with haloes in this realm any more than they are in any other. Anyway...I thought the idea of 'senior missionaries' had gone out of fashion these days."

"Not to me," Jenny said quietly. "I respected you...both of you. I was glad to come up here...to have this opportunity to work under you...learn from you...."

"Jenny...you need to understand the situation between me and Margaret...." began Julian, but Jenny cut him off.

"I don't want to hear it, Julian," she said, "I think we'd better...."

Suddenly her voice and composure broke. She turned abruptly and started to hurry up the hillside toward the Bible school.

The Triangle Again

Julian stood quite still, watching her until she disappeared into the trees.

When he reached the compound, some thirty minutes later, it was to find that Jenny had collected up the first band of waiting students and driven off herself in the first land rover. He had not known she had a national driving license.

He arrived home about nine in the evening. He saw the land rover Jenny had driven, neatly parked in the drive. The children were in bed and Margaret was sitting sewing in the living room. When she saw him, she got up.

"I've kept some supper for you," she said.

"Thanks."

He went to wash and then sat down automatically at his place at the table, while Margaret put a slice of bacon-and-egg pie in front of him and went to make tea.

"Jenny's left," Margaret said when she returned with the tea.

"Left?"

"Yes. She had a friend in the town—a Peace Corps girl. She's spending the night with her, so's to get the early bus in the morning."

There was silence.

"She left me her notes and things to hand on to anyone you thought could take her place."

He seemed incapable of speech.

Margaret sat in her usual place, at the other end of the table, and poured out the tea. She had a sudden vision of their life in the coming twenty, thirty years: day after day, facing each other across the table, having family prayers, discussing the weather, the shopping, the

The Triangle Again

children's education, maintaining the façade of a marriage because the cultural patterns of their life and work admitted no other way.

She had dealt with Jenny kindly. The girl had appeared shocked and shaken. Margaret had not asked, nor had Jenny divulged, what had occurred at Dneifan. When Jenny had announced her intention of leaving that evening, Margaret had at first been reluctant to let her, thinking that a night's rest might calm her down; but Jenny had been determined, and in the end Margaret had helped her. She had driven her to her friend's house and seen that she had a bus ticket.

There remained Julian.

She understood a little about the blow it had been to his pride. She thought maybe later he would find ways to think about it that would make it more tolerable: perhaps even come to think it was Jenny's fault for encouraging him. Later still, perhaps, he would search for spiritual lessons in the whole thing, perhaps come to be sorry for what he had done to Jenny, and to her. But she found herself at the moment almost indifferent to that.

Suddenly, loud in the stillness, came the noise of a drop of rain on the tin roof, and then, in the distance, a roll of thunder. Both of them automatically looked up. Rain! The drought was over. There was another drop, and another...soon a steady pattering. There were shouts in the distance as the people welcomed the end of the long drought.

There was drought too in their marriage, thought Margaret. It would be good to think that maybe now life would come to their marriage as it would come now to the earth beneath them, but she doubted it. Sometimes a couple could get so far apart—who had said that quite

The Triangle Again

recently? Must have been Julian—that they never... really...get together again. She got up.

"I'll see that the shutters are closed in the children's room," she said, and left Julian still staring at his bacon-and-egg pie and the cooling tea.

Chapter 9
Heartbreak

"Mummy, do we *have* to go back to school?" Fair-haired, and small for his thirteen years, Philip swung on the wooden posts of the verandah. "I like being at home with you and Dad."

Irene was used to this by now, which didn't prevent it hurting but did provide her with an answer.

"No, you don't have to, Darling, but if you didn't, you'd get very behind with your education. You know that it's for your own good that you go."

"Peter was crying a lot last night," volunteered Philip. "He doesn't want to come."

Irene felt tears threaten at the back of her eyelids, but answered with an attempt at firmness. "It's Peter's first time to be away from us, so of course he'll find it hard. You'll have to look after him, so he won't miss home too much."

"Bet he'll cry on the plane," said his brother gloomily. "Lots of kids do."

"Mrs. Irene...?" The tall, black figure of one of the local church elders and the mission compound chief

Heartbreak

stood at the bottom of the verandah steps and clapped his hands politely.

Irene put down her last-minute sewing of name tapes and got up.

"Greetings, Chief Owaya," she said, smiling at him. "Won't you come in?"

He did not smile back.

"Oh dear," she thought. "Something's offended him again."

"I have come to say that I am leaving the mission," the man announced with dignity.

"Is...is something wrong?" she said, going down the steps to him, since he had not accepted her invitation to come into the house. "My husband will be back presently. Perhaps he...."

"It has become obvious to me that you and Mr. Jeff do not truly care about us," Chief Owaya said, as if it was a carefully prepared speech. "Your lips say one thing but your heart does not feel it. You have not got our interests at heart."

Irene, standing in the hot sun with the flies around her, began to feel a little faint.

"Please, Chief Owaya, won't you come into the house?" she said. "Let's talk over what is bothering you. It must be a misunderstanding. Come inside and have a drink with me and the children. Mr. Jeff will be back very soon."

To her horror, she heard a note of appeal in her voice. Owaya was a difficult and touchy man, but he was invaluable to them. He managed all the compound workers, dealt with government officials with ease, and generally got them out of many difficulties. Jeff would hate it if she quarreled with him.

Philip was watching them.

Heartbreak

"Mum, I'm thirsty," he said.

"All right, Darling. I'm coming," Irene said, watching Chief Owaya stalk proudly away.

Over lunch she said to her cook, one of the Bible School students, who generally knew what was going on, "Do you know what is the matter with Chief Owaya?"

"He is angry that his cousin's children are not free boarders in the mission school," the student said readily. "He says no-one ought to pay anything...that the mission ought to feed all the students free."

"Mum, when are we going on the picnic?" little Peter asked in rather a quavering voice. He was trying to act bravely in a way that was nearly breaking Irene's heart.

"When Daddy gets back," said Irene, when a new thought struck her. If Owaya was really set on being difficult, Jeff, when he returned from the evangelists' class he was taking, would have to spend the afternoon trying to sort out that matter and wouldn't be able to take them on the promised picnic to the waterfall. And this was the boys' last afternoon. Tomorrow they would leave on the local morning plane for the capital city and then school in England. Was their last afternoon, so difficult for them all, going to be made worse by the fact that Jeff couldn't spend it with them? She felt a black rage against Owaya in her heart, and said to Peter, "But it's your favorite pudding, Darling. We had it especially. Why don't you want it?"

"I just d...don't," said Peter.

"Cry-baby...." began Philip, but stopped at the look on his mother's face.

She summoned all her courage. This time tomorrow the awful day would be over.

Heartbreak

"Now look, boys. I just want to pack up the cakes I baked this morning for you to take on the plane. Then we'll choose which of the beads and other things you're going to take to Granny and Grandpa. By that time, Daddy will be here, ready to take us out."

As the time passed without Jeff, she began to pray fiercely, "Lord, please give us this one unshadowed afternoon with the children. Lord, don't let Jeff hear about Owaya until tomorrow."

Then Jeff came.

"Hi, kids! All ready for off?" he said and swung Peter into the air. "You're going to be playing football this time next week," he told him. "After all the practice we've had, you should be really good."

He looked over at Irene and saw her white, smiling face. "All set for the picnic?" he said cheerfully. "You know, I bet we see that leopard down there today. Want to take the binoculars with us, Phil?"

"Oh yes!" Philip dashed off to get them.

They were going down the steps ready to pile into the land rover, when Irene saw Chief Owaya and other men approach Jeff. She could not bear it and ignored them, helping Peter into the back of the land rover and wedging the picnic basket so it did not fall. Jeff stood still, listening to a long complaint. "Oh, no, no," thought Irene. "Oh, don't let him start a long discussion now." She saw him glance at her and deliberately she looked away. Then she heard him say, "My boys are leaving for England tomorrow, Chief Owaya. I must be with them this afternoon. I will speak with you tomorrow."

"Unless the matter is settled," said the Chief with hauteur, "I will leave tomorrow also."

Another long pause. The children's voices were heard:

Heartbreak

"Daddy's going to take me to the *top* of the waterfall today." That was Peter, boastfully. Then Philip, scornful, "Huh. No-one could get right up there...."

"They could too...."

"Couldn't!"

"Could!"

Irene breathed a silent prayer and heard Jeff say quietly but firmly, "This afternoon I must spend with my family, Chief. I'm sorry. I suggest you wait a day. Nothing is gained by doing things in a hurry."

Chief Owaya looked furious, but Jeff turned his back and got into the car.

"Right, kids! Off we go! Ten cents for the first one to see a monkey!"

Next morning, in the stillness of the hot airstrip, Irene waited with the children for the plane that would take them away from her. Her face was haggard, but she talked calmly and cheerfully of inconsequential things. In a little group nearby, the Chief waited with his wife and a group of people to see them off. They would be going by the same plane to the capital city where, no doubt, they would try and make trouble for Jeff at the mission headquarters. Jeff had tried to speak to them, but the Chief had simply ignored him. Peter was red-eyed and silent, Philip talking boastfully to try and pretend he didn't care.

The plane came, bumping on the grass of the airstrip. There followed more minutes of bright conversation while some boxes were unloaded from the little plane and other stuff loaded on. For Irene it all seemed to be going on in slow motion, like a nightmare from which she could not wake up. There was the call for passengers. Peter flung his arms around his mother.

Heartbreak

"Mum, I don't want to go! Mum, I want to stay with you!"

Irene bit her lip until it bled, and smiled, saying cheerfully, "Darling, it's not forever. A year is soon past and you'll be back before you know it...and, you know, if ever you're sick and need me badly, Mummy will come right away."

Peter began to cry, in gasping sobs, holding onto her as if he would never let her go. But here Jeff took over. He gently lifted him away from her and took his hand.

"Come on, Pete! Philip's on the plane already, keeping you a seat. Guess the pilot will let you go right up front and see how the plane flies, won't you, Sir?"

The British pilot, standing near, played up gallantly.

"Sure. You can hold right on to the stick in the front if you like, Peter. Come on. I'll show you the way."

"No! No! No!" screamed Peter.

Jeff picked him up, and that was the last view that Irene had of him, carried in Jeff's arms onto the plane. Now she was at a distance, she let the tears run unchecked down her face.

"Oh God...lover of little children...care for them...."

Jeff appeared. He was white but perfectly under control, and he ran down the steps to where Irene stood.

"He's OK," he said. "He's in the front seat, this side. Wave at the front window."

The plane door had shut and it taxied to take off. Jeff and Irene waved as it moved slowly forward, gathered speed, lifted, and bore away their children. Then Irene's knees gave way and she hid her face, sobbing, on Jeff's shoulder. He helped her to the land rover.

Suddenly he heard his name called. He looked up, over Irene's head, to see, to his surprise, Chief Owaya with his wife. He had been oblivious of any watchers of

Heartbreak

the previous scene and had not noticed that they had not, after all, boarded the plane.

"Why...Chief Owaya?" he said. "Did you change your mind?"

The Chief looked different: more humble, more friendly.

"I'm not going," he said in a low voice. "I thought you didn't care for us, but now I have seen the agony it costs for you to send your children away. If you can bear that, just to stay here and help us, I know your love can be no greater." And he strode off.

He had spoken in front of a group of people. Looking at them, Jeff saw tears on many faces. He could not speak, but helped Irene into the land rover and they drove back to the suddenly quiet mission house.

Chapter 10
Death of a Cow

She was dead. The soft, brown eyes had rolled up once toward Michael, kneeling beside her, and then glazed over. Michael got wearily to his feet and went slowly over to his house to strip off his sweat-soaked clothes. For most of the hot, tropical night, he had fought in vain for the cow's life.

Later that morning he went over to the office of Mr. Elijah Akore, the African Project Manager. He was kept waiting twenty minutes and then shown into the big, carpeted office where Elijah worked.

"So you have come to tell me that we have lost the best cow?" Elijah said, without asking him to sit down. "That makes the third cow dead in the last month, Mr. Ratcliffe. The Diocesan Synod will want some explanation."

"You know these cattle are dying of ticks," Michael said tiredly. "I've been telling you we must buy dip for them for the last three months."

He tried not to mind standing like a schoolboy in front of the little, fussy manager who had, from the

Death of a Cow

start, manifestly enjoyed his authority over the young British graduate.

"I thought I had made it plain to you, Mr. Ratcliffe," said Elijah, folding his hands on the polished desktop, "that you were alone responsible for animal welfare. It is your job to see what is needed and to get it."

"Without money?" demanded Michael. "I have asked you constantly for money to buy the dip."

"The money given me for this project," said Elijah tightly, "is church money. I cannot use it without careful consideration of the needs of the whole project. In the six months you have been here, you have asked for vaccines, dip solution, fertilizer, maize and extra labor. Your predecessor did not make such demands."

"My predecessor was not trying to keep ten Jersey cows on a few acres of tick-infested scrub!" replied Michael, tired and exasperated. "Nor was he expected to run this farm at a profit to benefit 'church funds'! He resigned three weeks after you came, Mr. Elijah, and I can see why. You're a set of thick, incompetent fools, who don't know the first thing about farming!"

He had gone too far and knew it. Elijah's face darkened. He stood up.

"I find your manner offensive, Mr. Ratcliffe," he said. "I have noted from the start your critical and unfriendly attitude. It is not what we expect of a Christian missionary. I will speak to your superior."

Michael left the office, furious and frustrated, and drove to one of the distant fields where he leant for a while against a fence, trying to cool his rage. So much for his fine ambitions as a new missionary! "Getting on with the nationals" they called it in missionary books. He recalled the first letter he had received from a Mr. John Davey about this job. "We are praying,"

Death of a Cow

Mr. Davey had written, "that a young, single agriculturist will hear the call of God to work in this church project under the leadership of Mr. Elijah Akore, a dedicated spiritual leader."

And now? Michael had found the project dying through lack of funds, badly managed and underequipped. He had found in Elijah only a dedicated rascal, misspending the project funds. And now he would have to explain things again to Mr. Davey, who had initiated the project.

He was invited to lunch at the Daveys' house. They were an elderly couple, their children in England. They were kind, saintly, loved by the nationals, and, to the young agriculturist, they were about as likely to understand his problems as someone from another planet.

"You see, my dear chap," said Mr. Davey, leaning back in his chair and putting the tips of his fingers together, "our African brethren need to feel that you have confidence in them. Of course you are meeting difficulties. If there weren't difficulties, you wouldn't be here."

Mrs. Davey, fat and comfortable, poured out the tea.

"You know, Michael," she said kindly, "John and I have been wondering if there is something that is not helping you spiritually. We've felt recently that maybe you aren't quite right with the Lord. You do realize that we're only speaking to you in love. We do want to help you, don't we, John dear?"

Michael looked at her in despair.

"I suppose I may be spiritually rather dry," he said at last. "But I am trying. It's only that I feel sometimes it's up to us to face facts and do something about them, rather than waiting for God to do it for us."

Death of a Cow

He saw a text hovering in the air and hurried on. "I wonder how much you really know about Elijah?" he said. "Do you know, for instance, that...."

He was checked by Mr. Davey's upraised hand.

"Do you think I haven't heard these complaints about Elijah?" he said gravely. "None of us is perfect. I must tell you, Michael, that I think your own behavior has been much at fault towards Elijah. He has never been a problem to us. The trouble is that you young missionaries are unwilling to admit that Africans can lead anything. You must learn to submit to authority. Remember that the Bible says...."

"Mr. Davey," Michael interrupted. "Elijah is spending the funds you give him on drink!"

There was a hostile silence.

"You have no justification for that remark, Michael," Mr. Davey said finally. "Elijah is a trusted servant of the church."

"You shut your eyes to it," said Michael in a low voice. "You live up here in this lovely house with your flower gardens and cats! Of course everyone shows their best side to you when it is you who hand out the money! You may have started this project, but you have no more idea of what it is like to work in it than my grandmother!"

For three days Michael and Elijah studiously avoided each other. Then, to his surprise, Michael had a summons from the bishop of the diocese, Bishop Daniel Muwendi, asking him to call to discuss how some evangelists could get some elementary training in agriculture. Michael had only seen the bishop once, on his

Death of a Cow

arrival, but he retained the memory of a kind, intelligent face and a gentle, loving manner. He wondered briefly if the bishop would help him; or would he expect him to sort out his problems through the mission elders.

Next day, he drove to the city and parked outside the bishop's modest house. A servant showed him into the study and Bishop Daniel, alone, got up to receive him. Michael took his hand, but the bishop spoke first.

"What's the matter, Michael?"

Michael looked up, startled and suspicious.

"Why, Sir? Have you heard something about me?"

"I have heard nothing about you since you came," said the bishop, waving him to a chair. "That's partly why I wanted to see you. I asked you what the matter was because you look so tired and strained."

Michael looked down at his hands. "It hasn't been very easy," he said. "But why should I bother you with my problems?"

Bishop Daniel smiled at him and sat down opposite.

"Tell me," he invited. "Perhaps I can help."

And Michael told him. The bishop did not interrupt. When he had finished, there was silence for a moment or two. Then Michael said in a tone which he tried not to make bitter, "Well, say it. Tell me I've got a wrong attitude to your people; I'm not showing true love; I'm a guest in the country and I have to submit; I've got no more difficulties than anyone else."

Bishop Daniel spoke slowly, "I have never, myself, found it much help to pretend a situation doesn't exist," he said. "I have known for some time that Elijah was not the right man for the job."

"But you appointed him!" exclaimed Michael.

Death of a Cow

"No. Mr. Davey appointed him. Elijah grew up on Mr. Davey's mission, and he wanted one of his own men in charge."

"But can't you dismiss him?"

"I could, of course," agreed the bishop. "But it is not really my duty to do so. If the Synod and the project authorities both accept him, I should not interfere without being asked to do so."

Michael buried his head in his hands. "Then what can I do? I can't go on like this!"

The bishop sat still, looking very kindly on the young man.

"You think over one or two things," he said. "May I tell them to you?"

"Here we go," thought Michael. "More of what-I-should-have-done and what-I'm-not-doing!" Then he felt ashamed. He knew something of Daniel Muwendi from what others had told him. This was not a man shut away from life. This was a man who had suffered, who loved his people dearly, who knew from within all the struggles of emerging Africa. Whatever he offered would not be trite evangelical phrases emptied of meaning.

"Go ahead, Sir," he said.

"You say you can't go on," said Bishop Daniel. "That means one of two things must happen. Either the situation must change, or you must change. In this case, we can pray that Elijah may be truly converted and changed, or that the Lord transfers him to something somewhere else. Perhaps that will happen, but, in my experience, it doesn't happen very often. So let us assume for the moment that the situation will not change."

He paused for a moment, but Michael was silent.

Death of a Cow

"Now," the bishop went on, "the crops are doing badly, cattle are dying. You are being blamed for it, when in fact the fault lies elsewhere. Now, as far as the actual farming is concerned, remember that—however you dislike it as a farmer—the death of a hundred cattle cannot be compared with the loss of one human soul."

Michael flushed. "I know that," he said. "But...."

"But you naturally want to do a good job," finished the bishop for him. "I know that and I thank you for it. That leads me to the second thing: if it is important to do a good job for the Lord, it is even more important to be a good man for the Lord. Have you let your resentment at Elijah destroy your own peace and communion with God? If you have, then that is the true harm he has done you."

Michael got up and walked to the window.

"Go on," he said.

"To be blamed for something we have not done is galling to our pride," Bishop Daniel said gently, "but it is something Jesus knew all about. We should not expect life will be easier for us than for Him. Remember, you are only really responsible to God, and He knows the truth. Isn't that enough for you?"

"So I let Elijah walk over me?"

"So, for the moment, when necessary, you let Elijah walk over you. God will deal with him better than you can."

The bishop rose and came over to Michael where he stood by the window. They faced each other, the African and the white missionary, and it was the missionary who bowed his head.

"I'll try," he said. "I'm sorry I haven't done so well."

"You have done well," the bishop said, "in being ready to talk to me about it. I promise I'll try and drop

Death of a Cow

some hints to the authorities. In the meantime, remember that we need not let another's behavior influence ours; no one should ever have the power to harm our own relationship with God."

Michael went back. In the afternoon, he met Elijah face to face.

"I'm sorry I spoke as I did the other day," he said bluntly.

Elijah smiled patronizingly.

"That's all right, Michael. You're a young man still and a young man gets angry quickly. However, I hope it won't occur again."

Then Michael experienced a miracle. Fury rose in him like a wave, but died before it ever broke. He was left smiling with genuine affection at Elijah.

"Not if I can help it," he said.

For Further Thought

The yardstick
1. Do you agree that, because life is involved, Westerners should be slower to hand over medical responsibilities than, for example, church responsibilities?
2. What do you think of Peter Roxborough's comment that there is a difference between a moral principle and a cultural standard? What tests could you apply to distinguish between them?

The strike
1. What do you think about the various views expressed in this story concerning the differences in living standards between the missionary and the national Christian?
2. Would you have handled the situation at the school differently from Bill Underwood?
3. Do you think Ledda had any justification for his retort on page 52, "It is the Christianity you have taught us!"?

For Further Thought

An axe at the roots

1. Do you think Archdeacon Rassa right when he says that for the moment there can be no working side by side in the African church?
2. What changes do you think Rhonda will make in her own behavior if she goes out again to Africa as a teacher?
3. Consider for a moment the pressures on any white missionary who controls the giving of money to others, in view of the aphorism that power corrupts.
4. Is gratitude something we cannot really live without?

Between the lines

1. This story really involves a breakdown in communication. Discuss where and how the breakdowns had occurred.
2. Do you think it is true that if missionaries have to "find their own support" the best speaker will end up with the most money?
3. Do you think every missionary should be an evangelist?

The triangle again

1. What special stresses applied to the marriage of Julian and Margaret that most married couples would not have to cope with? Had either of them made those stresses worse in any way? What could they have done to lessen the tensions created?
2. How much sympathy do you have with Jenny?
3. Why do you think neither Julian nor Margaret came up with the conventional answer, "Let's pray about it"?